Organizational Dilemmas

Organizational Dilemmas

Robert I. McLaren

Faculty of Administration
University of Regina

JOHN WILEY & SONS

Chichester · New York · Brisbane · Toronto · Singapore

Copyright © 1982 by John Wiley & Sons Ltd.

Library of Congress Cataloging in Publication Data

McLaren, Robert I., 1940–
  Organizational dilemmas.

  Includes bibliographical references and index.
  1. Organization. 2. Management. I. Title
HD31.M384   658.4   81-19745
ISBN 0 471 10155 9   AACR2

British Library Cataloguing in Publication Data

McLaren, Robert I.
  Organizational dilemmas.
  1. Decision-making 2. Management
  I. Title
  658.4'03   HD69.D4
  ISBN 0 471 10155 9

Phototypeset by Input Typesetting Limited, London
and printed by Pitman Press Limited, Bath, Avon.

What a dilemma!

Should I dedicate this book —

to my parents, who gave me a love for the written word;

to my wife, who promoted my knowledge of organizations; or

to my children, who taught me that there are so many questions that have no answers?

I am indebted to Mrs. Shirley Sax for the typing and re-typing of the drafts of this book, and to Mr. Dave Weir for the preparation of the charts and drawings.

Contents

viii

List of illustrations

CHAPTER 1

Introduction

The Greeks had a word for it — dilemmatos. The derivation was di + lemma, meaning 'two premises.' Their mythology has given us the phrase, 'between Scylla and Charybdis,' between the six-headed monster, Scylla, on one side, and the whirlpool of Charbydis on the other. All the great sea-voyages of the Greeks — the Argonauts, Ulysses, and Aeneas — had to traverse this terrible strait between the two evils. It was a dilemma as to how to navigate it successfully without foundering on either side.

Although Scylla and Charbydis have faded into the past, dilemmas are still with us today. Indeed, one can say accurately that they will be always with us. As long as mankind attempts to create order from chaos, to organize and build, to defy entropy, dilemmas will exist. For dilemmas arise naturally from the very act of trying to achieve purposes or objectives. Dilemmas arise because we can rarely if ever achieve two goals simultaneously. One goal has to be pursued at the expense of the other. We keep away from Charybdis only to draw too close to Scylla; so we veer away from Scylla and find ourselves entrapped by Charybdis. In modern organizations, we might emphasize human relations and supportive friendliness only to find production targets being missed; so we make a concerted drive to be harsher and more disciplined so as to increase production only to find our employees leaving to work elsewhere. It is not just difficult to maximize two goals simultaneously; in the context of dilemmas, it is impossible. We cannot both eat our cake and have it, too.

Furthermore, if there are more than two objectives that we are trying to obtain, the task is even more hopeless. Peter Drucker has suggested that businesses have the following set of objectives:

(1) marketing;
(2) innovation;
(3) human organization;

1

(4) financial resources;
(5) physical resources;
(6) productivity;
(7) social responsibility; and
(8) profit requirements.[1]

To maximize the returns to all of these simultaneously is impossible, as several pairs are mutually exclusive. For example, a marketing strategy that attempts to give each customer a custom-made object is immediately in conflict with a productivity strategy that lowers costs through mass-production. Or, an organization may build up its financial resources at the expense of allowing its physical resources to fall into disrepair. It is difficult, if not impossible, to maximize both simultaneously, and thus a dilemma is created. The firm can maximize either, but not both. Which is to be chosen — Scylla or Charybdis?

As well, the passage of time exacerbates the dilemmas. Goals change and new procedures are adopted, but in the vast majority of situations the new objective can only be achieved at the expense of the old one. Automobile manufacturers in the early twentieth century that changed from high-quality, hand-made cars to low-quality, assembly-line production portray this well. This is the dilemma of modern organizations and modern management. It is the intent of this book to illustrate the scope and variety of these dilemmas so that modern managers can come to realize the limits of their actions.

There is already some recognition of dilemmas in administrative literature. For example, Peter Self has devoted a full chapter of his book, *Administrative Theories and Politics*, to a consideration of some dilemmas in public administration. And indeed, as he indicates, many other chapters in that book deal 'unofficially' with issues or dilemmas.[2] However, the reader is left by and large to ferret out these dilemmas from the surrounding material. In contrast, this present book focuses solely and totally on organizational dilemmas. As well, on the American side of the Atlantic, John Aram has written a book, *Dilemmas of Administrative Behavior*. While he devotes every chapter to the understanding of dilemmas, he focuses on only one topic — those that a decision-maker confronts as an individual. In contrast, this book attempts to be more comprehensive, suggesting that many dilemmas arise from the organizational structure itself. As a result, there are far more organizational dilemmas than Aram appears to envisage. However, this author agrees completely with Aram's perspective that 'choice as well as knowledge is the nature of administrative behavior.'[3] No matter how much we may do research into cause-and-effect relationships, someone is ultimately going to have to decide first what values we are trying to achieve before the 'knowledge' can be implemented. From these values arise our dilemmas.

Thus, this book is written in the spirit established by Christopher Hood in the mid-1970s. Hood, in *The Limits to Administration*, attempted to divert organizational theory away from its concentration on better and better ways for doing things.[4] Rather, he demonstrated what a 'perfect' organization, the supposed goal of so many modern theorists, would require, and then showed how unapproachable was that perfection. In fact, he showed not only that it is unapproachable, but that it should be unapproachable if we desire a democratic society of educated, decision-making individuals. This book is written in the same vein, although it avoids normative statements as to what *should* be done. It attempts to describe and explain the consequences of the important dilemmas that modern managers face daily. It is not totally comprehensive because new dilemmas arise continually whenever our goals and values change, and any listing would soon be out of date. However, it does profess to include all the important organizational dilemmas, be they private or public sector ones. In this way, it is hoped to follow Hood's attempt to provide rationality, objectivity, and understanding to the field of management. To recognize that there are limits to what organizations can achieve, to recognize that dilemmas are inherent to the organizational milieu is to recognize that it is inefficient in time, money, and energy for modern managers to attempt that which cannot be done.

The term, 'organizational dilemmas', has been chosen advisedly as being more inclusive than 'administrative' or 'management' dilemmas. It is considered that 'organizational' includes 'administrative,' but the reverse is not true. Some of the dilemmas arise from structural considerations, the static positioning of people and objects; some of them arise from the dynamics of administering or managing people and resources. The term, organizational, includes both the static and the dynamic. However, it must be admitted that the division between the two is considered an arbitrary one by many writers and may be satisfactory only to this author.

In any case, the emphasis is on organizational dilemmas and not personal ones, even if the latter do arise from one's work. Personal dilemmas, such as whether to be a 'yes-man' or to adopt a more independent stature, certainly abound within organizations and are certainly important to the people involved. However, they have been omitted from this book as the focus here is on the dilemmas that arise from the situations of managing other people, not oneself. Once again, though, the distinction may seem arbitrary to some people.

What is not arbitrary is the book's avoidance of false dilemmas — that is, dilemmas in which one goal is not worthy of modern managers and modern organizations. For example, it has been suggested that managements face the dilemma of treating their employees like mature, rational human beings with particular needs and abilities or treating them like robots and dismissing them when they fail to conform to the requirements of the machine or assembly line. This is a false dilemma for the second approach is not worthy of modern managers. There is no valid choice between responsible objectives in this situation. It is not worth anyone's time and energy to investigate such false dilemmas as if they were legitimate quandaries.

The dilemmas that have been chosen for this book are not particularly original with the author, and indeed there is no pretence to make anyone believe that they are. Most if not all of them have appeared elsewhere in management literature, and many have been noted by several writers. What is intended here is that these dilemmas be gathered into one place so that modern managers can recognize the overwhelming impossibility of trying to solve for all times all organizational problems. There are limits to administration, limits to what organizations can achieve. These limits exist naturally in the state of things and can only be surmounted at the cost of giving up other goals and objectives. The author believes that it is time that modern managers, and students or would-be managers, recognize this and do not waste any more time, money, and energy trying to attain the unattainable.

The dilemmas have been arranged in the following manner. First, those dilemmas dealing with centralization and decentralization have been considered to be of such overwhelming importance, and surrounded by such overwhelming confusion, that they have been isolated as a separate chapter and given special prominence. It is hoped that the confusion surrounding the use of the terms will be removed in this manner. The next chapter deals with dilemmas found in the structures of organizations, the natural results inherent to man-made objects. Their static nature contrasts with the dilemmas in the following chapter which deal with managerial considerations arising from the everyday dynamics of administering people and organizations. The final chapter deals with dilemmas confronted by the organization in its externally-oriented relationships with its environment.

It should be noted that the author uses the terms, 'management' and 'administration,' as synonyms, and considers an organization to be any group of people working together for a commonly-held purpose. Thus in general, the dilemmas illustrated in the book apply to all types of organizations. It is recognized that there are significant differences between public-sector and private-sector organizations or among universities, unions, and hospitals, for example; however, these differences do not usually negate the dilemmas chosen for the book. Although there are significant differences between types of organizations, there are also significant similarities, and dilemmas are most likely to fall into the latter area.

There is a tendency in Western civilization, perhaps due to its Grecian heritage and especially Aristotelian logic, to seek 'The Golden Mean' and try to find the right balance between the twin prongs of any dilemma. The author cautions the reader against this, and suggests that a lesson can be taken from Mary Parker Follett in this regard. In 'Constructive Conflict,' Follett stated that there were three main ways to resolve a problem — domination, compromise, and integration.[5] Follett arranged them in this manner as being in ascending order of utility to the people trying to resolve the conflict.

The most desirable, integration, was said to involve the search for an alternative outside the two possibilities present in the conflict. However, in the context of these classic dilemmas, it is unlikely to be a fruitful search or people would have found it years ago. A dilemma seeks to obtain both goals simultaneously, not eschew either. In Follett's examples of integrative solutions, the problems were always with conflicting means, not ends. Thus, when she suggested an integrative resolution, it was always a different set of means to achieve the agreed-upon end.

For example, she cited an instance in a Harvard library when she did not want the north wind blowing on her, but another person wanted the window open. The integrative resolution was to open a window in an adjoining room, so that both got the fresh air they desired, but she was not in a draft.[6] In all her examples, there are no conflicts in objectives, only with the ways of achieving the objectives.

In dilemmas, though, it is the ends themselves upon which there is no agreement. Two sets of ends, two different goals, are desired, both equally; neither can be given up. Integration is not a likely resolution under these conditions, as this book will illustrate frequently.

The natural tendency is therefore to turn to compromise — balance. However, as Follett suggested, this is often a less-than-desirable solution as neither side achieves its real objective. The compromise becomes a short-run expedient and pressure soon builds for each side to pursue its original objective. With the exception of the environmental dilemmas, in the following chapters managers will find only rarely a suitable balance as a solution to a particular dilemma. Dilemmas are very much either-or choices, zero-sum games, situations in which domination results, at least the domination contained in pursuing one objective at the expense of the other.

For those who find domination inherently distasteful, the consolation is that, as time passes, the dominant objective becomes taken for granted while the forsaken objective seems ever more important. In time, a decision is made to pursue the latter as the benefits of the former are either forgotten or ignored. Thus, the domination becomes reversed. Anyone who has experienced the periodic changes of an organization first centralizing decision-making authority, then decentralizing it, and later recentralizing it will recognize the validity of the above assertion. The organization is caught in a dilemma. No one has yet derived an integrative solution and a compromise would only produce chaos. We cannot both centralize and decentralize authority for the same decision simultaneously. Domination must be chosen, but it will only be a short-term solution until the pressures for the missing objective overcome the system.

The cynic would say that these organizational 'solutions,' so often introduced by teams of outside consultants, are merely expedients that will soon require a reversal or flip-flop to the original situation, and the cynic would not be wrong. Organization and administration are not ends in themselves, they are only means to an end. If in fact the group does not have just one end or goal, but many, and these are conflicting or evolving or both, then it is absolutely certain that there will be dilemmas amongst whatever goals are chosen. As will be demonstrated in this book, integration would be lovely, but unlikely; compromise will reach a balance for some dilemmas, but is just as likely to produce chaos for others; domination is then all that is left, one goal to take precedence over the others.

Now who in the organization should decide what that one goal should be — or is that a dilemma in itself?

Notes

1. Peter F. Drucker, *An Introductory View of Management* (New York: Harper & Row, 1977), p. 89.
2. Peter Self, *Administrative Theories and Politics* (2nd ed.; London: George Allen & Unwin, 1977), p. 247.
3. John, D. Aram, *Dilemmas of Administrative Behavior* (Englewood Cliffs, N.J.: Prentice-Hall, 1976), p. 8.
4. Christopher C. Hood, *The Limits to Administration* (London: John Wiley & Sons, 1976).
5. Mary Parker Follett, 'Constructive Conflict,' in *Dynamic Administration*, ed. by Henry C. Metcalf and L. Urwick (New York: Harper & Row, 1941), p. 31.
6. Follett, 'Constructive Conflict,' p. 32.

CHAPTER 2

Centralization and decentralization

Centralization and its counterpart, decentralization, are probably the two most over-used terms in organizations today. Not the least reason for this is that, as will be shown below, the two terms together describe at least four different organizational circumstances. The British are ahead of the North Americans in coining different terms, such as devolution, to describe some of these circumstances. However, the new term does not erase the dilemma in the circumstances, and nor does it really take us very far when the counterpart of such a word as devolution is still centralization. We are left with the situation that demands for centralization or decentralization generate more studies, debate, and printed words than any other concerns in modern management. Therefore, to understand the dilemmas in centralizing or decentralizing organizational operations, it is first necessary to define the four circumstances that the terms describe.

The first of these circumstances is the locus of decision-making, or where resides the authority to make significant decisions within the organization. The second situation refers to the geographical location of the organization — is everyone located in one building or are there units of the organization scattered around the city, the country, or even the world? The third situation refers to the provision of common services, such as the purchase of materials or the use of computers or even the maintenance of accounts. Should these be handled from a central location or decentralized amongst the various departments or branches? Finally, it has been suggested that the decentralization concept can also be used to describe situations where staff advisors or non-line managers make significant decisions.[1] Where the first circumstance mentioned above dealt with vertical decentralization in the organization's hierarchy, this fourth circumstance can be said to deal with horizontal relationships.

It is important to note that these four situations are quite independent of each other. An organization may be centralized in some respects and decentralized in others.

	CENTRALIZED	DECENTRALIZED
1. LOCUS OF DECISION – MAKING AUTHORITY		
2. GEOGRAPHICAL LOCATION		
3. PROVISION OF COMMON SERVICES		
4. USE OF STAFF EXPERTISE FOR DECISION – MAKING		

Figure 2.1 Types of centralization

For example, a government social services department may centralize its decision-making authority vertically at the top of the branches, may decentralize its operations through regional field offices, may centralize its computer facility at its head office, and may decentralize its decision-making authority horizontally by allowing staff branches to direct line branches. On the other hand, an organization involved in applied research may vertically decentralize its decision-making to the individual researchers, may centralize its operations in one laboratory, may decentralize its computing facilities through giving each researcher a computer, and may horizontally centralize its line-staff decision-making through giving no authority to the staff personnel. But neither of these are models of what is done typically within that industry. One would be equally likely to find a social services department decentralizing its decision-making throughout the branches, or a research lab that had centralized its computer facilities. All that can be said is that, mathematically, there are sixteen possibilities. Furthermore, one common service, computing facilities, may be centralized, while another common service, secretarial staff, may be decentralized. Each aspect requires its own decision by the organization; the only certain thing is that the chosen decision will reflect a dilemma.

Finally, in looking at this set of dilemmas, we should avoid considering centralization and decentralization as a dichotomy, an either-or situation. Instead, the four circumstances represent continuua, ranges of possibilities extending from centralized to its opposite, decentralized. What we are discussing are situations where things are more or less centralized, more or less decentralized, rather than absolute positions. This is especially true of the decision-making circumstances because we cannot define what constitutes an 'important' decision or a significant decision, except in relation to a particular organization. Otherwise, what is important to a small organization, perhaps because it involves £1 million or 20 employees, may be insignificant to a multi-national conglomerate. Thus, the small organization might decide that decisions about that matter should be centralized while the larger organization habitually decentralizes it because of its non-importance to their total operations. Even in the case of geographical location, there are gradations of centralization and decentralization. Having all locations within one city is more decentralized than having them all in one building, but is more centralized than just having them all in one country. How centralized or decentralized is the situation determines the extent and size of the dilemmas to that particular organization.

a. Locus of Decision-making Authority

To place the authority for making all the important decisions with one person is the ultimate in achieving coordination within an organization. This is centralization at its most extreme. This type of coordination should ensure that all the decisions are consistent with each other, have continuity with decisions made in the past, and are in line with the policies and objectives of the organization. Furthermore, it enhances accountability by placing the blame for poor decisions squarely on one person. To achieve these virtues of coordination, consistency, and accountability, it is not surprising that many modern organizations attempt to centralize their decision-making authority.

An example of this type of extreme centralization is illustrated by a situation drawn from a reformatory system in the late 1960s. At two o'clock one morning, it was discovered that a teenage boy had escaped from the reform school and was presumed to be making his way across the countryside. The director of the reform school could take no action until he had first phoned the headquarters of the social service department and obtained permission to go out and search for the boy. Headquarters was thirty miles away in this case and the director's superior was, of course, not there, but had to be awakened at home.

In time, permission was received and the search began, but the boy was never found.

In this case, centralizing the decision-making authority at headquarters achieved its three goals. Accountability for the decision to spend money on the search was ensured. Consistency with past search procedures was maintained to ensure that neither a harsh search using dogs nor a half-hearted search was undertaken. This maintained objectivity and excluded personal considerations that might have arisen since the boys usually made friends or enemies of the reform school officials very quickly. Finally, coordination with the rest of the social service system was maintained as headquarters would not now have been taken by surprise were they to initiate a contact with this particular reform school. On the other hand, the search took so long to get away that the boy was never found and never returned to the school.

Centralized decisions take a much longer time to get made than decentralized ones. The latter can be made immediately by those at the scene and action can be gotten underway quickly. Moreover, when decisions are decentralized to lower levels in the organization, it both makes use of the expertise that is locally available and motivates the subordinates by demonstrating the faith of top management in their abilities. Related to these is the fact that decentralizing decisions also helps to train the future superiors in the organization. An organization can scarcely expect its senior officials to make good decisions if it has never allowed these people to make important decisions when they were juniors. 'Practice makes perfect.' Decentralization of decision-making authority, therefore, has the virtues of reducing the time required to make the decision, of making use of expertise throughout the organization, of motivating those who want the responsibility of making decisions, and of training subordinates in decision-making.

But can the senior officials be sure that these decentralized decisions will result in the best for the organization? Will the decisions be consistent with those in other departments? Will they adhere to the organization's policies? Will they be consistent with past decisions? Will they even be correct decisions? Practice may make perfect, in time, but how many improper decisions will the top managers suffer while the subordinate is learning? And who is then accountable when the incorrect decision is costly or inefficient or both — the subordinate or the senior official? Why should a senior official allow the subordinates to make important decisions when that official knows that he or she will be held accountable? These are the questions that create the dilemma for the officials in the organization. Of course, it is well known that no one person in an organization can be totally responsible for any one important decision. Information must come to that person from other people and the implementation of the decision must be done through others. Yet, the sports pages of the newspapers tell us daily that it is the coach, not the players, who gets sacked. Senior officials are aware that they are expected to be accountable for both good and poor decisions.

So organizations swing back and forth from centralization of decision-making authority to decentralization. They are in a dilemma between coordination, consistency, and accountability on one side and speed, local expertise, motivation, and training on the other. In the above-mentioned reformatory system, authority for search decisions was decentralized to the directors of the reform schools in the early 1970s. As a result, when a boy escaped under the new system, some of the directors made the decisions to conduct the search themselves, some called meetings of their staff to achieve a collegial consensus as to what to do, some still called headquarters for advice. In manning the searches, some directors kept within their budgets, but did not find as many boys; others hired local farmers to help, but overspent their search budgets each year. Some used dogs; others would not dream of using a dog to track a human. By the end of the decade, the senior officials of the department of social services had the feeling, the impression, that they did not really know what was happening throughout the system, that they were not really in charge of the reform schools. It worried them. They were in a quandary as to whether they would be better off if they were to return to the old ways and centralize the decision-making authority again, and they finally decided to do so in 1980.

Organizations try various combinations to solve the dilemma of where to locate decision-making authority. All combinations are sub-optimal in time because the two sets of virtues cannot be achieved by any one organizational design. The best answer for any organization is to decide which set of virtues is more important to it, locate the decision-making authority to achieve those virtues, and then forget about the problem. To shift back and forth from centralization to decentralization or to try to combine the two by centralizing important decisions and decentralizing unimportant decisions is merely to create morale problems. Subordinates know the difference between unimportant decisions and important ones, and they know that a radical change in philosophy back to centralization indicates that top management has lost faith in them. If the organization stays with either the one or the other, centralization or decentralization, it will soon gather to itself the type of work-force that can function best under that philosophy. Employees who shun decision-making responsibility will leave decentralized situations, and employees who seek that responsibility will flee the centralized workplaces. In 'solving' this dilemma, the organization can do no better than to assist its employees to find the situation with which they are most comfortable.

b. Geographical Location

In this situation, the dilemma does not concern the question of whether or not the organization should have field offices, or branches scattered around some territory. It is assumed that these field offices exist and that the organization is therefore geographically decentralized. The dilemma arises from the problem of maintaining adequate communication links between the head office and these field operations. Adequate communications will help to ensure coordination and conformity throughout the field and also allow queries and initiatives from the field to be properly processed or utilized by headquarters.

There are two distinct bases for organizing these adequate communications. Unfortunately, they each achieve different goals and thus create a dilemma for any organization trying to establish its communication links with the field. (At least one writer has suggested that there are four distinct bases, but a close examination of the four will reveal that two of them are merely variants of the basic two.[2]) The basic two methods can be called the Specialist Method and the Generalist Method.

In the Specialist Method, each Field Office communicates directly (by visit, telephone, or letter is not important here) with the individual department at Headquarters. If the Field Office needs advice from the Accounting Department, it goes straight to the department at Headquarters to obtain that advice. Or, if the Marketing Department at Headquarters wants to localize its new selling campaign in a particular area, it communicates directly with the individual Field Office for that territory. Two-way communication without an intermediary is paramount in this method. The advantages to this method are

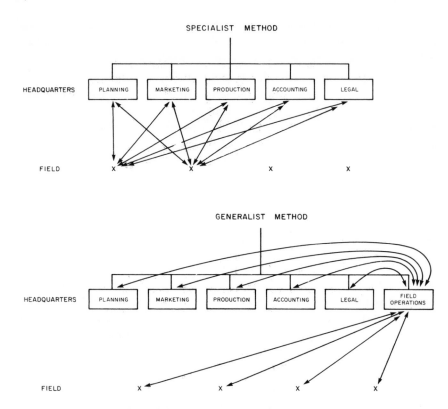

Figure 2.2 Headquarters-field relationships

several. Of prime importance is the speed with which queries can be handled. There is no intermediary to slow down the processing of the communication. Furthermore, without an intermediary, there is little chance that the communication will be garbled and reinterpreted. Finally, the two parties, the Headquarters department and the Field Office, will be communicating about the specifics of the particular situation, not in generalities that attempt to cover all the Field Offices so that both parties have to try to decide what the communication was intended to mean.

However, how well will this Specialist Method work when the Field Office does not know with whom it should be communicating at Headquarters because duties and responsibilities there are often changed? Or how well will it work when the query involves two or more of the Headquarters departments? And how will the query be handled if the responsible individual at Headquarters is on vacation or out of the office for some reason? And how is the overworked Field Office to react when several of the Headquarters departments initiate new proposals or programs or training sessions for their particular functions all at the same time? It is at times like these when the lines of direct communication are overloaded that the Generalist Method is introduced to reduce the load and solve the problems.

In the Generalist Method, a separate department, bureau, desk, or office (here called Field Operations) is established at Headquarters with total responsibility for all communication to and from the Field Offices. Now there is coordination so that no Field Office is inundated with visits or directives from Headquarters. Now there is consistency in that all Field Offices are treated similarly by each functional Headquarters department. Now there is no problem of queries and messages from the Field going astray or being directed to the wrong person or department; Field Operations knows exactly who is doing what at Headquarters and who should be contacted for any situation and who should not.

Of course, now there is less speed as well in getting answers to questions. And now it appears that Field Operations is sometimes misinterpreting the query or directive and sending it to the wrong place. And it also appears that Field Operations does not have as total a responsibility as it claimed because one of the Headquarters departments, in the name of expediency and claiming that its needs were more important than that of Field Operations, just by-passed Field Operations and went directly to the local Field Office. Perhaps it is time to do away with Field Operations and get back the speed and clarity of direct communications? Is Field Operations just a worthless appendage at Headquarters that cannot pay its way? Thus does management have another dilemma on its hands.

An example of this dilemma occurred in the Public Service Commission of Canada in the 1970s. Prior to 1974, the recruitment of university graduates for the Canadian public service followed the Specialist Method. Each of the four classes of people needed by the departments, Executive, Administrative, Science and Technology, and Social and Economic, were recruited directly on the university campuses by the individual departments. From the Headquarters perspective, it was judged that each department knew best its own requirements and knew best what students could satisfy them. So each department went out to the campuses on its own. However, from the perspective of the students on the campuses, the procedure was a hodge-podge. A student would have to submit an identical application to every different department in which he or she was interested. The departmental representatives sometimes arrived on the campus on the same day and scheduled interviews at the same time, or, just as bothersome, arrived four or five months apart with the student then being asked to make a decision on the offer from the first department long before the interview with the second department had even taken place. Furthermore, if a student had applied for more than one class or position with the same department, he or she would have to have multiple interviews with that department as it appeared that the different departmental representatives for the four classes did not talk to each other. Overall, the image of the Canadian public service among university students was not encouraging.

Therefore, a decision was made by the Canadian Public Service Commission in 1974 to introduce the Generalist Method for this situation. The Public Service Commission established its own office, the Public Service Recruitment Program (PSRP), and undertook all campus recruitment for these four classes through this office. Now the students had only to make one general application and were only interviewed once on campus. The results of the interview were circulated to all departments and students would hear from these within a few months. From the student perspective, the system appeared efficient and the public service seemed attractive. However, from the perspective of the departments, the new system was inferior. The general application was not considered to be detailed enough to cover the range of requirements for all the individual needs — that is, natural sciences for the Science and Technology class, social sciences for the Social and Economic class, commerce and administration for the Administrative class. Furthermore, the results of the interviews were not enlightening as the generalists in the PSRP did not have the expertise necessary to ask the right questions for each of the classes. Finally, the PSRP, in its processing of the students, emphasized the future potential of the applicant as a career manager in the public service whereas the departments wanted the stress to be put on the present skills of the applicants with regard to a current job vacancy. The departments stated their particular short-term needs, but the PSRP reinterpreted them in the light of the long-term needs of the whole public service.

Resolution of the dilemma was suggested through two different attempts to compromise. On the one hand, each PSRP recruiter could attempt to become a specialist for one of the four classes. However, this would then require 3–4 trips by the PSRP to each campus and some students would be subjected to multiple interviews. The image of the public service would once again be lessened.

On the other hand, each PSRP recruiter could be accompanied to the campus by a departmental representative for each of the four classes. Now the student would face an interview panel of as many as five persons, or some of these five could sit around outside waiting for the next interview. Again, the image of the public service would be lessened by the obvious waste of manpower. The problem would also arise as to how to coordinate the needs of the PSRP interviewer representing the PSC and the one or several departmental representatives. Who would be the mission leader? Furthermore, two departments might both need Science and Technology graduates, for example, but they would need them for different positions with different requirements and the problem would arise as to how the one departmental representative for the Science and Technology class was to be chosen. Either compromise would lessen the image of the public service for the students and still leave the departments displeased because their particular individual requirements were ignored.

In general, compromise is most likely to be chosen to resolve this dilemma, but its results are rarely satisfactory. The suggestion is usually made that the Specialist Method be used if the Field Office originates the bulk of the communications since speed and directness seem to be the paramount needs. If the Headquarters originates most of the communication, then the Generalist Method is usually recommended to ensure coordination. However, if both Headquarters and the Field are initiating the queries and proposals, a combination of the two methods can only lead to chaos. This will happen because, if the Field Office cannot contact the necessary person, it will turn to Field Operations and disrupt that flow; and it will happen because individual departments at Headquarters will decide that their needs are so important that they will by-pass Field Operations and go directly to the Field Offices. Like water, employees will seek continually to work their way around and through whatever barriers have been created. Once again, the only lasting 'solution' to this dilemma is for the organization to decide which method satisfies its present requirements best, institute it, and adhere to it until such time as requirements have so changed that the other method must be introduced. With luck, that time may never come.

c. Provision of Common Services

It is theoretically possible for any manager at any level within an organization to handle every function required by the work unit that he or she is directing. The manager can hire all the subordinates, and fire them, review their performance and create training programs. The manager can handle all the accounting requirements, all the planning of production, all the supervision, all the legal work, or at least can ensure that it is done by someone in the unit. Many a small business is a good illustration of this situation.

On the other hand, organizations can decide that all those elements that are common to many or all units within the organization should be handled by one common or central unit of its own — for example, a personnel department, a computer department, a purchasing office, a legal section, a printing unit, an accounting section, an internal audit group, a marketing group, a secretarial pool. The variety of these common services is only limited by the type of organization. If the organization provides any of these services from a common or central location, that service is said to be centralized; if, as in the previous paragraph, each manager or work unit provides the service for itself, it is decentralized.

At first glance, it would seem that all the advantages to the organization lie with centralized services. A further look at the actual practices of most organizations would seem to confirm this. Centralized services appear to be most efficient and economical as they make use of the 'economies of scale.' With a centralized printing office, for example, the organization need only purchase one or two large machines and the staff can be both kept to a minimum and kept busy as all the other offices send their work directly to the printing office. As well, technological changes in the printing industry could be more readily adopted as they would affect only one location in the organization. Finally, the centralized printing office would provide greater career possibilities as the employees, all specializing in various aspects of printing, would have more opportunities for personal development and promotion, either in the centralized unit of the organization or in another organization when the openings occurred. These advantages for a centralized unit would tend to exist for any type of common service, be it an accounting department, a personnel department, a computing department, or a secretarial pool.

On the other hand, while it is easy to see the merits of economies of scale in the abstract, it is often more difficult to find them in reality. If a marketing department wants a run of 1000 copies of a promotional letter, that run size is not going to change no matter whether the printing machine can handle 1000 in an hour, or 10,000. Thus, to send the order to a centralized printing office with its large machine that can handle 10,0000 copies per hour may not produce any real economies. That is, any money saved by the lower per unit costs of the large machine may be negated by the extra costs of having to have a delivery system to and from the centralized office and by the delay necessary while the marketing department awaits its turn in the schedule of the centralized printing office. A centralized unit cannot help but extend the turnaround time for any job, be it a printing order, a letter to be typed, a purchase of supplies, or just advice from an accountant, a lawyer, or some other expert. Where time means money to an organization, the proposed economies of scale from a centralized unit must be weighed against the extra costs of the extended turnaround time.

Furthermore, if the centralized equipment ever breaks down or when it requires its periodic servicing, the organization is in an extremely vulnerable position. Were the equipment to be decentralized throughout all the departments, then a breakdown or a maintenance check in one piece of equipment would affect only that one department where it occurred. The other departments could continue to function normally and one of them might even have some slack time on its equipment that it could offer to that one department. Of course, both the capital and the operating costs of all these smaller pieces of equipment might well be greater in total than that for the large machines in the centralized unit, and they would be probably less efficient, too. However, the equipment for the decentralized approach should be more suited and adapted to the particular needs of each individual department and that factor, coupled with its ready availability, may outweigh any supposed efficiencies of a centralized unit.

This argument is just as valid if it is people and not equipment that is being discussed. Having an accountant or an accounting section in each department results in greater suitability and availability of this expertise than there would be if the department had always to seek out a centralized accounting unit somewhere else in the organization. However, the uniformity obtained for the organization by the centralized accounting unit may be considered to be more important than the desires of each department for individualized service. It is a true dilemma because each approach can satisfy different goals.

It is sometimes suggested that the centralized approach is too susceptible to 'empire-building.' That is, the centralized unit acquires too much control over the provision of the service to the organization and its concentration of expertise allows it to obtain new machines and additional staff that may not be totally justified. Any complaints by the other departments would be 'suicidal' because the centralized unit creates its own schedules of whose work will be done and when. While there is no doubt that this illustration can become reality all too easily, a well-run organization can establish measures to check the tendency. Furthermore, the 'empire-building' can occur just as easily in the decentralized approach. In this approach, each department can use its own budget to purchase specialized equipment or hire additional staff that it cannot justify economically. The department then offers its expanded capabilities to other departments or to new types of clients outside the organization, or even convinces top management that it can better handle a project than can another unit. However, none of this has anything to do with the dilemma. Empire-building is a function of human nature, not of conflicts in goals. The empire-builder may use a conflict in goals as an opportunity to build up an 'empire,' but many other employees will not.

The realization that some employees are empire-builders may be the 'bottom line' in causing an organization to adopt a decentralized or a centralized approach to resolving the dilemma of providing common services. However, empire-building, itself, is not inherent to the dilemma. For example, a university computing department operated as a centralized service throughout the 1970s. Each faculty or department would take its needs to the Computing Services unit and would be assigned an analyst-programmer by the Director of the unit. The authority of this Director increased handsomely throughout the decade as he alone determined the purchase and scheduling of the computer equipment, priorities among the users, and, most importantly, the quality of the assistance provided by his unit since not all the analyst-programmers were equally competent. By the end of the decade, enough resentment had been created in the faculties and departments that they were able to press their case with the senior administration of the university. However, since the Director was by no means derelict in his duties, what grounds could be used for breaking up his empire and removing him as an obstacle?

The solution decided upon was, in the guise of individualized service to the users, to assign the analyst-programmers on a permanent basis to each of the users. Thus, the Business Office would now have its own analyst-programmer, as would the Registrar's Office, the Library, the Faculty of Science, and so on. 'A decentralized approach to providing this common service,' was the announcement given to the public. However, the public was not informed what the real problem was; it was merely led to believe that this approach would better achieve the organization's goals, whatever those were.

The computing equipment was still centralized, but the intellectual heart of the Computing Services unit, the analyst-programmers, was taken away and the Director was left with little of his empire. Furthermore, the unit was placed under the authority of another unit which then took charge of the scheduling, the priorization, and the purchase of new equipment, and the former Director was made an Assistant Director in this new unit. As was expected, the former Director quit the university within days of the reorganization and moved to a new city. The example illustrates how top management can appear to use the very objective requirements of the different organizational goals that are contained in this dilemma to overcome a very subjective problem within the organization. Indeed, one can only wonder how long it will be before the university now recentralizes the analyst-programmers on the pretext of obtaining efficiency and economies of scale.

What remains is a dilemma between a decentralized approach to providing services that are common to the needs of many units, and a centralized approach. The former is much quicker for the individual unit, much more suitable in satisfying unique or particular requirements, and makes both the unit and the organization much less vulnerable to malfunctions. However, the decentralized approach can also be a duplication of resources throughout all the units and thus be inefficient; it is wasteful when the decentralized capacity is sitting idle because the unit does not have enough work to occupy it fully; and it can be a 'dead-end' situation for the employees who become invaluable to the unit in providing the service.

Thus, the centralized approach can be instituted to overcome these disadvantages. However, the advantages of the centralized approach are only the disadvantages of the decentralized approach, and vice versa. The centralized unit can produce economies of scale, can reduce idle capacity, can create a career system for employees, can lead to uniformity in operations throughout the organization. But it will also be slower in response time for the individual department, will demand that the individual department conform to the requirements of the centralized unit, and will cause confusion if not chaos in the organization when it breaks down or malfunctions.

To ensure that the centralized services does not dominate the user departments but operates as a true service, it is often suggested that the user departments should pay for the centralized services. Since the market system is believed to promote efficiencies between firms, this suggestion takes the market system inside the firm and expects the same results. The individual user departments will transfer some part of their operating budgets to the budget of the centralized service department for the requisite services. If they are not satisfied with the service of the centralized department, the users will take their business, and their budgets, elsewhere. This potential to go elsewhere will keep the centralized unit in check. On paper, it is a sound proposal; in practice, it has no validity. In fact, it merely creates a 'Catch-22' situation.

The 'raison d'être' of the centralized unit is to obtain economies of scale for the organization, as well as uniformity in operations, the elimination of idle capacity, and the creation of a career system. If the individual departments are not compelled to use the services of the centralized unit, then it is absolutely impossible for the centralized unit, or the whole organization, to achieve these goals. One might just as well adopt the decentralized approach and do away with the centralized unit. A true market system is, in effect, a decentralized system and therefore cannot operate logically in tandem with a centralized system. The recommendation to institute a market system can only aggravate the dilemma; it cannot resolve it. If the centralized unit is not serving the user departments, but dominating them, then it must either be removed or reoriented through changing people's attitudes. Introducing a market system only increases the total costs to the organization.

One suggestion for resolving the common services dilemma is to have a centralized unit in the organization and a representative of that unit in each individual department. This suggestion is impractical if equipment or machinery is the heart of the common service as it merely aggregates all the disadvantages of both approaches. It is similar to the Catch-22 situation above. For example, it makes no sense to have both one large printing press in a central location and a smaller one in each department if economies of scale is the goal. The employees of each department will rarely use the centralized equipment.

However, the suggestion is more reasonable, at least on paper, if the service is purchasing or legal advice or something involving people only. Unfortunately, in reality, it too does not solve the problem. All it does is to remove one dilemma, the provision of common services, by substituting for it another dilemma, that of the unity of command. The problem now becomes that of who directs the representative — the centralized unit or the particular department? This dilemma will be discussed below in Chapter Three. In addition, the resolution may also create the dilemma of communication between the centralized unit and the decentralized representative, the geographical location dilemma that was outlined in the previous section. Finally, it will certainly be more expensive than either the centralized or the decentralized approach.

Domination would appear to be the only sensible resolution to this dilemma. If the work can produce the benefits obtained from the economies of scale, or if it can be scheduled with enough lead time to satisfy the requirements of a centralized unit, or if organizational conformity is paramount, or if it requires some technical expertise that is not readily available, then it would seem that the centralized approach should be used. However, if the job lots are small, or time is of the essence, or if almost any employee can handle the work required, then the decentralized approach is recommended. However, the work of most organizations will require the virtues of both approaches. In these cases, the organizations can only priorize their needs and choose one or the other approach, knowing full well that they will not satisfy all of the people all of the time.

d. Use of Staff Expertise for Decision-making

When the organization has centralized any or all of the possible common services, and it is a rare organization that has not centralized some, another type of dilemma is created. In effect, the organization has established a staff group to service the line departments or branches, and the organization must now decide how much decision-making authority that staff group should have vis-à-vis the line groups. Since organization charts are drawn typically with the line elements in the centre and the staff elements out to the side and slightly above (like vultures wheeling around a carcass?), this dilemma is referred to as horizontal centralization and decentralization whereas the first dilemma examined in this chapter is usually entitled vertical centralization and decentralization. It involved only the line elements.

A definition of the line is: all the people who are directly involved with the production of the goods or services which the organization makes for its clientele. This would include everyone from the chief executive officer at the top to the most junior worker at the bottom. The staff people would then be defined as: those people who advise, assist, or serve the line people, and thus allow the latter to get on about their work. The staff people can be said to be indirect contributors to the production. However, since these definitions define the category by the type of work being performed at any one moment, it is obvious that a person could be both line and staff depending upon the nature of the particular task being performed. For example, an accountant could be a staff person offering advice to a person in another department and also be a line person when performing the duties of an internal auditor evaluating the production process. In any case, both administrative literature and organizational usage have accepted that there is a distinction between line and staff operations, although it is usually conceded that the distinctions are not always clear in either theory or practice.

In fact, many would suggest that the terms, line and staff, be rejected as they do more harm than good in creating status distinctions amongst employees. This contention is that everybody either contributes to the organization or they do not. If they do not, they should be fired. Those that are not fired are neither line nor staff, but employees. However, this contention does not eliminate the fact that some employees are directly involved in the production of the goods or services and some are advisers and assisters of these people, as are the common service people, for example. Thus, whether we like it or not, there are two types of employees in the organization, and they cannot be evaluated and analyzed in the same manner; therefore, whether one calls them line and staff, or oranges and apples, is irrelevant. Contending that they do not exist is merely wishful thinking. They do exist, and so we might just as well refer to them as line and staff, as usage suggests.

It is also accepted in both the literature and the practice that there are two types of staff units. A distinction is made between the units that provide common services — thus called auxiliary units — and the units that provide advice to the chief executive officer — thus called advisory units. However, this distinction has no relevance to the dilemma under investigation, and indeed has little merit in practice. For example, when a budget officer makes the annual budget, is this the provision of a common service for the line departments, or is it giving advice to top management? It is a rare staff unit that does not provide both types of service,[3] and so the distinction will be ignored in this section. The formation of staff units creates the potential for these units to affect the decisions made both by top management and by the line units who use that staff service, and that is the topic under consideration here — who makes decisions.

The dilemma that arises from line-staff relations concerns the amount of authority that the staff have to make decisions that will direct the line in its operations. From the definitions of line and staff, it would appear that there is no cause for the staff to have any of this decision-making authority; they merely advise, assist, and serve. Both the reality of human nature and the rationality of creating a staff with special expertise, however, would suggest differently. As was illustrated in the previous section, a centralized common service leads to the development of specialized expertise. Does it make sense for the senior officials in the organization to deny the staff the authority to introduce this expertise into the line operations?

If the staff is precluded from exercising decision-making authority over the line, the situation is one of horizontal centralization; if the staff group can exercise this authority, decision-making authority is horizontally decentralized. (Either situation is possible with either vertical centralization or vertical decentralization within the line elements; the two areas are mutually exclusive and so can be combined to make four possibilities.)

The virtues of horizontal decentralization are that the organization: (1) encourages the development of specialist expertise within the staff unit; and (2) ensures standardization or conformity throughout the organization to the staff's recommended practices. The two are intertwined. In both cases, there is literally no rationality for creating a staff unit unless it has the authority to make and implement its own decisions. That is, why should a staff unit develop its specialist expertise if the line departments can choose to ignore it? Similarly, why should a staff unit establish policies and practices as a standard for the whole organization if once again the line units can choose to ignore the directives? A staff unit that is not horizontally decentralized, that cannot exercise decision-making authority over line departments, is a unit whose employees are frustrated, low-spirited, and most likely not well-qualified.

On the other hand, who knows better than the line department what actions it needs to take in light of its own budget, what personnel it needs to hire and at what price, what is the most efficient way to organize the production? What gives the staff people the right to constrain the line and force it into some standard mold? How can the line manager be held accountable for the line department if he or she must continually take directives from some so-called expert in a staff department? These questions arise quickly from the line units who would much prefer a situation of horizontal centralization, a situation where their expertise is encouraged rather than the staff's, and where standardization is foregone for the benefits of individualized initiative and adaptation. Again, the two are intertwined. For the line unit, a situation that is not horizontally centralized is one where the line manager is frustrated, low-spirited, and most likely not well-qualified. Whose morale is most important to the organization?

For example, many large organizations have a continuing need for in-service training of their employees. Since the need occurs throughout the organization and since much of the new knowledge is common to several departments, it is logical to place the responsibility for conducting this training in a staff personnel unit. This staff department can organize periodic training sessions to which the line departments will send those employees who qualify for that particular session. At the session, the staff personnel people outline uniform procedures which the employees are expected to introduce within their departments and so assist top management to coordinate the organization. This horizontal decentralization of authority to the staff personnel unit cannot help but allow them to feel important.

However, the line manager, who has had to release employees to the training session, perhaps jeopardizing production deadlines, or whose individual procedures and standards will be overruled by the new generalized information brought back by the employee, is not pleased by the system. This horizontal decentralization usurps that person's authority to make decisions. How can a staff personnel unit give proper training to employees drawn from a variety of departments and situations? It is analogous to the university lecturer who must generalize in order to make the material relevant to all the students.

Under horizontal centralization, the line managers could conduct the training sessions for their own employees themselves.

But do the line managers have any expertise in conducting training sessions? And do they have the time to prepare all the necessary materials? And would not several of the line managers be saying many of the same things to their particular employees? This seems like a wasteful and inefficient use of the line manager's time. Why does the top management allow this when it could assign the training function to a staff unit? Scylla and Charybdis are both monsters.

Most resolutions of this dilemma attempt to set down in black-and-white the division of authority between the line unit and the staff unit. The line unit will make such-and-such decisions for particular matters and each of the staff units will make such-and-such decisions in its area. Indeed, it is usual to find the organization proceeding through the following checklist of questions to resolve the dilemma for each major type of decision:

(a) who can propose a given kind of action?
(b) who is consulted on it?
(c) who decides?
(d) who is informed?
(e) who directs performance?
(f) who keeps records of performance?
(g) who analyzes and reports on performance?

This establishes a workable compromise. Indeed, it is akin to integration. Unlike most other compromises in management, it does not produce chaos. However, it does not produce heaven either. No one should be so foolish as to believe that the answers to the above checklist will leave both line and staff in perfect harmony.

For example, the fact that all line managers will be treated equally in having their employees hired by a common personnel department does not make any of them happy when they need a particular type of worker at a particular time and they do not have the discretion to hire that person. Similarly, just because the organization has decided that no line manager can reallocate the budget of his or her line unit without approval of a staff budget officer will not make all of the line managers feel better just because they are being treated equally. The constraints may be equal for all the line managers, but they are still constraints. These are examples of horizontal decentralization; it may be rational for the organization to introduce them, but it does so at the expense of the autonomy of the line. As a result, it will always be a compromise that leaves at least one side, the line, more dispirited than it would like to be. Moreover, to the extent that the staff unit did not gain from the resolution all the decision-making areas it desired, it will leave both sides dispirited. But such is the nature of compromises.

For this dilemma, domination makes no sense as an alternative. Both line and staff need a certain measure of decision-making authority or there is no justification for their existence. Accordingly, the question is one of how much authority for each side or authority over what areas. The resolution is achieved through compromise, but the organization should realize the morale implications of compromise and should recognize also that the passage of time may soon reintroduce conflict as the requirements and technologies change. As Follett suggested, compromises quickly result in both sides looking for new ways to gain the upper hand.

Notes

1. Henry Mintzberg, *The Structuring of Organizations* (Englewood Cliffs, N.J.: Prentice-Hall, 1979), pp. 185–86.
2. J. E. Hodgetts, *The Canadian Public Service* (Toronto: University of Toronto Press, 1973), pp. 226–29.
3. Herbert A. Simon, Donald V. Smithburg, and Victor A. Thompson, *Public Administration* (New York: Alfred A. Knopf, 1950), p. 282.

CHAPTER 3

Structural dilemmas

Throughout this chapter, and indeed throughout this book, it has been assumed that the organizational form is a hierarchy. That is, the structure of the public and private sector organizations where these dilemmas occur is composed of several levels or grades. In turn, these hierarchical levels are filled by employees who are considered to be superiors to the employees on the levels below them and subordinates to those people on the levels above. The hierarchical form of organization is the most common throughout the industrial world and may be the closest thing that mankind has to a universal organizing principle. Indeed, at least one writer, Herbert Simon, would suggest that hierarchy is natural to the human condition, not just because it is most common in organizations, which are after all only artificial constructs, but because it is the natural manner in which the human brain works.[1] Whether or not the anthropologists would refute this is not important here. What is pertinent is to recognize that hierarchy is the most common characteristic of organizational structures. More importantly, hierarchical structures contain within themselves the seeds of five dilemmas which will be the substance of this chapter.

An obvious reaction to that last sentence would be that organizations could eradicate these dilemmas by eliminating their hierarchical components. Indeed, this is the message of one organizational theorist.[2] However, it is the contention here that it is impossible to eradicate hierarchy, even if we wanted to. Nor is there evidence that we want to. As the discussion of the dilemmas will illustrate, hierarchy serves useful purposes as well as creating problems, and many people will prefer its benefits, no matter what problems ensue. Furthermore, there is much to be said for the perspective that hierarchy is an immediate consequence of all attempts to organize. Even such organizational forms as cooperatives, unions, or representative democracies where the membership is supposed to lead the elected official soon evolve into hierarchical pyramids where the elected official leads the members. Robert Michels noted this at the start of the twentieth century and called it, 'The Iron Law of Oligarchy.'[3] It is just as evident at the close of the twentieth century in the operations of trade unions, professional associations, cooperatives, and democratically elected legislatures. It would appear that 'hierarchy ye shall have always with you' and so it is the obvious assumption for this book.

a. Bureaucracy

Although all organizations have a hierarchical structure, it does not follow from this that they all operate in the same manner. Some organizations may be very insistent that each hierarchical level exercises a tight control over the level below it, but other organizations may well require that the lower hierarchical level operates with a great deal of freedom. The dilemma that arises for the organization from this was described in the last chapter as the locus of decision-making authority. As well, in some organizations, it may not even be obvious which hierarchical level is the superior one. For example, in a research organization composed of one hierarchical level made up of researchers and a second level consisting of a manager or director, it is just as natural to envision the director as the subordinate level providing administrative services to the researchers as to think of that person as the superior level giving directives to the researchers. The same phenomenon occurs in representative organizations. Is the union leader on a superior hierarchical level to the members, or a subordinate one implementing the wishes of the union membership?

Where the organization follows the practice of insisting that each hierarchical level exercises tight control over the subordinate levels, the situation has come to be identified by the term, bureaucracy. In its original usage, bureaucracy referred to many more characteristics than just tight control. Most analysts of bureaucracies, for example, would also ascribe functional specialization, formal rules and regulations, a norm of impersonality, and administration as a life-time career to this organizational form. However, the term is being used here merely to characterize an organizational form that is geared to the production of standardized units, be those units cars on an assembly line, applications for unemployment payments, cheques from a payroll department, or anything else. In the 1960s when the concept of bureaucracy was under its greatest attack, both by the general public and by organizational theorists, bureaucracies were also referred to as antiquated, mechanistic, standards-oriented, and maintenance organizations. All of these terms are useful; they help to describe 'the beast.'

But is a bureaucracy such a beast after all? It is certainly correct that the term, bureaucracy, usually has pejorative connotations. It is also obvious that the attackers of bureaucracy, who called it antiquated, mechanistic, standards-oriented, and concerned with maintenance, were reserving the more chiliastic terms — modern, organic, innovation-oriented, and adaptive — for their preferred organizational ideal, whatever that might be. However, as the childhood taunt suggests, 'Sticks and stones may break my bones, but names will never hurt me!'

The merits of a bureaucracy lie exactly in its characteristics, disdained or not. A bureaucracy seeks to standardize its operations both for the benefit of the organization and for its clients. The organization benefits because it does not need continually to 'reinvent the wheel.' Procedures are established by the organization to handle all possible situations that may arise in its operations and all that is then required is for the employees to determine which situation is at hand and to follow the appropriate procedures. Rules and routines ensure consistency and conformity in the operations of the organization.

This benefits the clients of the organization as well. No longer does the client have to be concerned with the whims or idiosyncracies of the individual employee. The client knows that the treatment received is the same for all clients and no favouritism will ever be shown. Bureaucracy replaces the highly subjective, personal, 'rule of man,' with an objective, impersonal, 'rule of law.' Clients are now assured in advance of the treatment they will receive and they can make plans accordingly. They do not have to spend time 'polishing the apple' and hoping that they are successful in currying favour with certain employees. When clients are disdainful of bureaucracies, as often as not it is because they want everyone else to be treated uniformly, but they want special treatment for themselves.

However, social commentators repeat and repeat that change is the only thing constant in our modern industrialized world. If this is true, how can bureaucracies possibly envision in advance all possible situations and the procedures necessary to handle them? Business competitors produce new products or new variations on old products; clients adjust their behavior to accommodate social changes, such as higher interest rates, and thus alter their needs for social services; employees realize that the organization will benefit if a client keeps returning to buy more products, so they adjust the procedures somewhat to accommodate the individual client. All of these types of changes occur naturally and are desired by both the organization and society in general. How can the organization be both bureaucratic and flexible?

The answer, of course, is that it cannot, at least not easily, and this is the heart of the dilemma. For example, in business, we see this dilemma in the form of the production group versus the marketing group. The former wish to reduce the number of products to as few as possible, standardize their production, and thus keep costs to a minimum. The marketing group, on the other hand, want as wide a choice of products as possible so that the client or the customer will buy something from the firm no matter how varied is his or her taste. The marketing group has little concern with how the products are produced and at what cost as long as the customer can afford them.

In the public sector, the dilemma is illustrated within an immigration department, for example, by the need to establish set procedures to handle all applications uniformly and impartially, and yet be able to respond quickly to sudden crises in world affairs that create distressed refugees and a need for compassion in accepting otherwise-unqualified applicants. As the attackers of bureaucracy suggested, the modern organization must be adaptive and flexible. However, one should not 'throw out the baby with the bathwater.' The modern organization also needs to be standardized and consistent if it is to keep down costs and treat its clients impartially. For all its supposed faults, no other organizational form has ever surpassed the mechanistic bureaucracy in producing the maximum amounts of goods or services at the minimum cost, and the citizens of industrial societies have recognized this.

The resolution of this dilemma appears to be simple and straightforward. Unfortunately, however, it is only a compromise. The resolution is to build into the organization both bureaucratic and adaptive elements. As matters become routinized and the benefits of standardization become obtainable, a bureaucracy is formed to handle them. But there needs always to be another element of the organization, at whatever level or point in the organization that top management decides is best, to react and adapt to changes in the environment of the organization. This adaptive element will likely place little or no stress on hierarchy and, indeed, was envisioned by the critics of bureaucracy as the ultimate replacement for all bureaucratic elements.

But these critics were wrong on two counts. It has already been noted that they were wrong because the bureaucratic element is necessary to produce maximum output at minimum cost. They were also wrong because human beings cannot continue to operate year after year in a totaly flexible, adaptive environment. This environment is one of continuous pressure and requires people to be continually on the alert. It is not possible for humans to sustain themselves in this manner as a career. Bureaucracy is both a relief, because it allows the individual to work without much thought about the work, and a reward, because it allows the individual and the organization to accrue the benefits of repetition. Practice makes perfect, and repetition is a type of practice. Thus, the organization needs both bureaucratic and adaptive elements. Domination is not a practical solution to this dilemma, and nor is integration as the goals associated with both adaptation and maintenance are desired by the organization, not something else that is outside these two concerns.

However, this resolution is only a compromise because it has done nothing to alleviate the tension caused by the two needs. Indeed, in demanding both elements, it has created tension. The adaptive element, to justify its existence, will be continually promoting new products, new practices, new procedures in the organization; the bureaucratic element, to attain its goals of minimum costs and maximum output, will be continually resisting the implementation of these new products, new practices, or new procedures. One can imagine easily the arguments that will ensue in the board rooms and committee meetings. The compromise is necessary to the continued existence of the organization — all organizations need both a maintenance mechanism and an adaptive mechanism — but a continual state of tension within the organization must result. This is not to say that tension is necessarily harmful and there should be no tension within an organization. Indeed, the contrary may well be preferred. It is only to say that the dilemma creates tension for the organization and there is no compromise that will remove it.

The tension that results from this resolution can be noted especially in the problem that results for the organization in its treatment of its employees. The set of employees that are involved in maintaining the bureaucratic elements will most likely be required to work: (1) standard hours (often the daytime hours to accommodate the general public); (2) in one location (a desk or a work-bench); and (3) under close supervision (to ensure standardization). For that set of employees, however, who are most concerned with the adaptive needs of the organization: (1) their hours of work are likely to be very flexible (including weekends); (2) they may or may not be at their work location at any given time; and (3) they are unlikely to have more than periodic consultation with a supervisor. Can the first set of employees observe this inequitable treatment without rancour?

For example, a programmer-analyst in a computer department may work very odd hours as a result of the time available to gain access to the computer or as a result of being called to the computer centre in the middle of the night because the computer has stopped due to faulty logic in the analyst's program. The analyst then works for 8–9 hours and decides to go home at 10:30 a.m., having put in a good day's work. But that is not what the bureaucratic elements of the departments see, nor the general public. They see only a person going out into the morning sunshine when they are confined behind a desk, or they see higher taxes or higher prices because employees do not appear to be putting in a full day's work any more. It is difficult to avoid comparisons if one feels slighted by the treatment received, and tension remains high no matter how thorough is the explanation.

In universities, the resolution is attempted within the same people. Teachers are made responsible for both the bureaucratic elements of lectures and seminars at specified times, and for the adaptive elements of research and writing and program innovation. However, this does not eliminate the tension. On the one hand, it is a rare faculty member who does not stress one element to the neglect of the other; on the other hand, if the faculty member does balance the demands successfully, observers are usually only aware of the bureaucratic operations and assume the faculty member is day-dreaming rather than thinking, sleeping at home rather than working at home, or wasting time in committee work. The tension is not necessarily reduced by combining the two elements in the same person. Furthermore, most organizations are unlike universities and would not have the potential anyway to combine the two elements in their employees. The dilemma will exist as long as the need exists for an organization to maintain stability while seeking innovation.

In the 1960s, largely as a result of NASA's Space Program in the United States, a new organizational structure, the matrix organization, was developed as an attempt to resolve this dilemma. Industrial firms with contracts to supply space equipment for NASA attempted to integrate this short-term, once-only requirement with their on-going, production line operations. Thus, the 'matrix' was created by the horizontally-oriented extraction of personnel from different operations, who would then work as a team on the space equipment, superimposed upon the vertically-aligned hierarchy that prevailed for the routine, continuing operations. Flexibility in creating the space equipment and meeting that one contract would be combined simultaneously with the maintenance of the firm through the continual production of its standardized items.

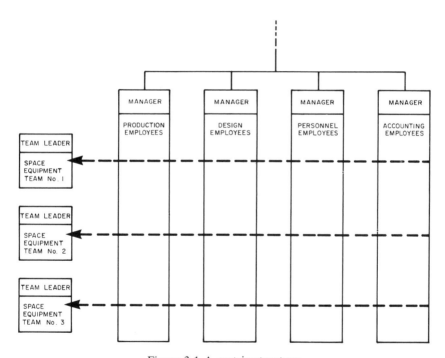

Figure 3.1 A matrix structure

However, like most compromises, the solution created as many problems as it resolved. Indeed, the fundamental dilemma between adaptive flexibility and continuing conformity was not resolved, but only highlighted by the matrix. Tension was built explicitly into the system where it had only been implicit before.

For the maintenance-oriented line operations, the managers and foremen found themselves losing some of their best workers to the space equipment team; they found deadlines and quotas harder to meet; they found it more difficult to get the required inputs for their production lines; and they found themselves with lowered status as the space equipment team became the 'darlings' of the firm.

But for the adaptive mechanism, the space equipment team, the matrix was not heaven either. The team leader had to negotiate with the line managers for personnel and resources to be released, and often failed to meet deadlines when the line managers used their *de facto* authority as controllers of the resources to balk the *de jure* authority that top management had assigned to the team. Furthermore, because the team leader basked in the new-found status, there was no incentive for that person to ensure that the contract was completed. If top management could not obtain another contract for the firm, completion of the contract could only mean that the team leader, and the team, would return to being 'nobodies' in the continuing line operations. Even if top management did obtain another contract, there was no guarantee to the present space equipment team that they would comprise the team for the new project. Finally, the people selected for the team usually had shown themselves to be above-average employees, successful in solving problems and managing themselves like professionals; they tended to resent any demonstrations of authority by the team leader, especially as that person was only their leader temporarily and would not be involved in decisions about promotions and other aspects of their careers. Thus, the team leader had to be a 'nice guy' to everybody, but if he or she was too nice, nothing would be achieved as both the line managers and the team would take advantage of the vaguely-defined situation.

Nor are the above problems confined to space equipment contracts. They exist wherever and whenever a project team is created from an on-going operation in order to provide an adaptive mechanism. The temporary project team, extracted from the line and superimposed upon the organization in matrix style, is one way to attempt to resolve the dilemma of bureaucracy. However, it can only be a compromise at best. It does nothing to alleviate the tension of the dilemma, and indeed may heighten it considerably. The tortoise envies the rabbit's speed and popular image, while the rabbit knows that the tortoise will outlast him. Neither is satisfied.

b. Authority

Hierarchy demands authority. That is, the hierarchical relationship of superior and subordinate demands that there be some mechanism to ensure the obedience of the subordinates to the superior. This mechanism is authority. In modern organizations, the concept of authority occupies an amorphous middle-ground between the concept of power at one extreme and the concept of influence at the other extreme.

Power connotes the ability to force compliance from subordinates through the use of physical punishments or sanctions. Its use is limited these days to rare situations, such as prisons and the military, and is becoming rarer each year.

Influence, the other extreme, connotes suggestion and advice from one person without the ability to insist on the compliance of the other. It is therefore a non-hierarchical mechanism and so, although prevalent and important in organizations, is not of immediate concern to the dilemma of authority. As long as hierarchy exists, one will not solve the dilemma of authority through an insistence on the use of influence. Influence cannot dominate a hierarchical situation. A superior may think that he or she is merely influencing the subordinate to do something, but the subordinate is always fully aware of the hierarchy in the situation.

The dilemma of authority is that authority can arise from two sources. Official authority, or legal authority, resides in the position and exists irrespective of who occupies that position. It may be created by statute or simply by the organization itself. In either case, it attaches an importance to the position which gives the holder of the position the legal right to require compliance from those whose positions are subordinate. This positional authority may thus be said to flow downwards in the organization; that is, it is created by superior levels and assigned as needed to lower-level managers in the hierarchy so that the latter, in turn, can deal with their subordinates.

However, positional authority is not the only source of authority for the holder of a position. It is not positions that give directives and demand compliance, but persons. A position may exist irrespective of the person who fills it, but that does not negate the importance of the person to the position. There are two aspects to the concept of superior — position and person — and therefore a second source of authority arises from the personal attributes and characteristics of the holder of the position. This personal authority, often referred to as working authority or leadership authority, flows from person to person, usually upwards from subordinates to their managers, and is largely beyond the control of the organizational superiors. It arises in the followers and is attached to the person, their leader, not the position, due to the leader's personal qualities and abilities. Personal authority is a relationship amongst individuals where followers recognize the superiority of a person; positional authority is a relationship amongst roles where superiors assign authority to a position and subordinates recognize the legitimacy of the position.

It is usual to think of personal authority as flowing upwards in an organization, from subordinates to their manager, but this is not necessarily the case. In the Vietnam War, a lieutenant might find himself out on patrol with three subordinates, one in charge of the radio, one in charge of the mortars and ammunition, and one to scout the enemy. Of a sudden, the lieutenant would find himself deserted by the three men fleeing back to camp. Did he then whip out his pistol and shoot the deserters in their backs to assert his positional authority? More likely, he realized that the man in charge of the radio had information from Headquarters and other patrols concerning the enemy's plans, the man in charge of ammunition knew what weapons were left to them at this point, the scout knew how close the enemy was and how many there were. The smart lieutenant would forget about his position and instead pick up his equipment and run back as fast as he could, too! Personal authority flows to the people we respect for their deeds, knowledge, or character, not for their positions. Thus, it may flow in any organizational direction.

As a momentary digression, the above distinction between personal and positional authority also suggests that it is impossible to delegate authority, contrary to the predilections of many modern organizational theorists and management consultants. Authority is either assigned to the position by superiors and therefore cannot be delegated away by the holder of the position, or else it is assigned to the holder by the followers as a personal attribute and also cannot be delegated away to any other person. Robin Hood might ask his men to serve Little John as they served him, but the men will not find the request an easy one to accept. What the men see in Little John is not what they revered in Robin Hood.

The responsibility to do something, along with the resources required to do it successfully, can be delegated by a superior to a subordinate, but not the authority for having it done or being account-able for it. The authority either resides in the position and therefore cannot be delegated away; or it resides in the person as a recognition by others and also cannot be delegated away, but only transferred by these others to someone else — if they so choose. Advisers and consultants need to be more explicit about what they mean when they suggest that managers learn to delegate authority.

For the organization, the dilemma that arises from the need for authority concerns the amount of insistence that should be made upon positional authority. Positional authority is inferior to personal au-thority in that it does not motivate the subordinates in a positive way. To insist on one's positional authority as the reason that some action should be taken is to admit that one has not been able to explain successfully to the subordinates the necessity, the rationale, or the benefits of the action. The declaration, 'We are doing this because I said so,' may put an end to the discussion, but it does not create a positive willingness in the subordinates to undertake the work. Their work will be a minimal effort. As long as sufficient work can be done to avoid the punishment, nothing more will be attempted. The insist-ence or reliance upon positional authority is an admission of defeat in one's superior-subordinate relationships.

If the superior can use personal authority to gain compliance from subordinates, if the superior can build a relationship with the subor-dinates such that the latter recognize the merits of the superior's wishes or directives and are desirous of fulfilling them, there is a positive motivation in the subordinates. Now the work will be well above any minimal level. This personal authority is created by dem-onstrations of responsible leadership by the superior, it can be created by the superior's permitting unimportant rules to be broken, it can be created by explanations of the necessity, rationale, and benefits of directives, it can even be created by peer-group pressure as subordi-nates convince each other of the superior's personal qualities. What-ever the reason that it exists, personal authority is superior to positional authority for increasing the motivation of the subordinates and the morale of the work unit.

However, from the viewpoint of top management, personal au-thority is less desirable because it is less controllable by the organi-zation. The more the lower-level managers rely on personal authority, the more autarkic are their work units. Top management no longer has control over these work situations; control has passed away from the organizational roles and framework and into the individual work units where the superiors and subordinates have established good interpersonal relationships. This is not necessarily harmful to top management nor the organization, but it does mean that top management has had to replace more rigid control mechanisms with an element of trust. There is nothing wrong with relying on trust to bond together the members of the organization. Indeed, it may well be the most preferable bond — as long as one can trust it.

However, where middle-managers rely extensively on personal authority, top management can only hope and trust that their middle-managers are achieving their objectives properly. Unless they have built their own relationships with middle management on a basis of personal authority, they have lost the capacity to insist on compliance. Because personal and positional authority arise from different bases, they are mutually exclusive. The more that one is used, the less is there a need for the other.

Top management is faced with a dilemma. To insist on positional authority throughout the organization enhances the control of top management and their understanding of how the organization is working; but the members of the organization may be complacent, relatively apathetic, and probably quite dispirited. Adaptability and innovation will be foregone and conformity and constancy will reign. If top management is not satisfied with that state of affairs, it can hire more dynamic and personable middle-managers and insist that these latter cultivate a reliance upon personal authority. To the extent that the middle-managers succeed in this, however, top management will have less control of the situation and will have to trust that the flexibility and diversity now being built into the organization are good for it.

And of course, it may not be. The personal authority may simply be created at the expense of top management, through ridicule of high-level directives, goals, and quotas, or by ignoring rules that top management does not consider so insignificant after all. Are the flexibility, diversity, and good interpersonal relationships really achieving more for the organization, or merely creating a country-club atmosphere in the work unit such that little productive work is done? Furthermore, what happens to the organization or the work unit if that middle-manager with all the personal authority decides to leave and go to a different organization? Should the replacement come from the ranks as a popular leader, or be brought in from outside the work unit, and what happens in the interim while the base of personal authority is being re-established?

To a certain extent, the use of personal authority is like tasting forbidden fruit. Having tasted it, one is usually not prepared to return to the old stuff. For the subordinate, having once been in a situation where personal authority underlay the relationship, to change to a situation where positional authority undergirds the relationship is to lower morale and create depression. The more the top management encourage the use of personal authority, the more vulnerable is the organization as the more difficult it becomes to retreat to an insistence upon positional authority. On the other hand, to never move very far from the pole of positional authority is to doom the organization to an impersonal, catatonic existence.

In a world of change and adaptation and one where subordinates need to be positively motivated, the only resolution of this dilemma is to move toward the pole of personal authority. However, the organizational leaders must recognize from the start that this may well increase tensions in the organization and may well create more problems than it eliminates as it becomes more difficult to control the various forces in the subordinates, the superiors, and the work environment. The resolution should be looked upon as being akin to riding a tiger instead of a donkey; one gets there more quickly, but it may be difficult to ever get off.

A corollary to the above dilemma occurs in the personal situation of the middle-manager. Whether foreman, supervisor, branch director, or whatever, he or she has been rightly called the 'man-in-the-middle.' These persons are caught between their own subordinates and their own superior. Should they enhance their personal authority by ingratiating themselves with their subordinates, an action that will probably weaken their relationship with their own superior, or should they cultivate their relationship with their superior, who after all has immediate responsibility for their promotions and career growth, and alienate themselves from their subordinates? It is difficult to serve two masters.

A classic example of the man-in-the-middle dilemma occurred in the design department of an airplane manufacturing company. When the occasion arose for selecting a new Senior Designer, the logical choice was to select the Designer who was both the most popular and the most capable of the existing Designers. The other Designers agreed completely with the selection and the Senior Designer began his supervisory duties with a great deal of personal authority and little need for the positional authority. For a long while, the Senior Designer remained 'one of the boys,' helping the other Designers with their work, meeting them regularly at lunch or after hours for a drink or bowling, and largely ignoring the other managerial people.

Eventually, the Senior Designer was called before his own superiors and asked when he was going to stop acting like a worker and start acting like a manager. His failings as a supervisor in planning and evaluating the work of the unit were shown to him and he began immediately to take corrective action. He now insisted that the Designers meet his schedules, solve problems themselves as they were paid to do, and stop bothering him needlessly either during work or after hours. The Senior Designer's personal relationship with his own superior increased rapidly, but his new insistence on a base of positional authority with his subordinates led some of the Designers to quit and move to a competitor.

Somehow, the 'man-in-the-middle' is supposed to balance these conflicting pressures and resolve this classic dilemma, but there is no simple way. The work of the superior is not the work of the subordinate, so that they both must have different interests and different roles. Personal authority is enhanced by the superior ignoring his or her own work and adopting the interests of the subordinates. This results in the work unit being a nice place for the subordinates and may result in greater productivity, but it may also mean that the organization is not receiving what it expects from either the superior or the work unit. For the organization to now insist on the requirements of its roles and positions may well bring the work unit and the superior into line, but will it do so at the expense of productivity and good working relationships in the work unit? It is a dilemma.

The dilemma between positional authority and personal authority is sometimes written as the dilemma between *de jure* authority and *de facto* authority. However, there is no consistent parallel between the two sets of terms and, indeed, the latter is not a true dilemma. *De jure* authority is the authority that exists because of a law or rule; in that sense, it is similar to positional authority. *De facto* authority is the authority that one has because of the reality of the situation, irrespective of the law. In the previous section, the matrix structure illustrated an example of the *de facto* authority of a situation being separate from the *de jure* authority. The *de facto* authority was not based on the followers' recognition of the leader's particular qualities;

it was based, as it is commonly, on the control by one person of the resources in a situation.

Thus, there is no dilemma between *de jure* and *de facto* authority because the two are not necessarily opposed. What one would hope is that the *de jure* authority and the *de facto* authority reside in the same place, and it is one requirement of organizational leaders to see that they do. When the two types of authority are separate, it reveals a failure on the part of top management, it does not illustrate a dilemma.

For example, throughout the first half of the twentieth century, the Federal Government in Canada gave the *de jure* authority for staffing the Public Service of Canada to the Public Service Commission. However, it gave the *de facto* authority for this responsibility to the Treasury Board which had control of the government's budget and expenditures. Like all these situations, *de facto* authority outweighed *de jure* authority and Treasury Board dominated the situation. The conflict between the two bodies was resolved finally in 1967 when an act was passed to give the Treasury Board the *de jure* authority for this responsibility that would support its *de facto* authority. The separation of the two types had been a problem, even a crisis, but not a dilemma, as no one had desired that the two types be split.

On the other hand, positional and personal authority do comprise a dilemma because they arise from two different bases, neither of which can control the other. Situations are at their best when positional and personal authority are congruent, but the leaders of the organization can only hope for this, they cannot make rules to insist upon it.

c. Span of Control

Whichever source of authority dominates, it will be reinforced by a limitation on the number of subordinates that are directly supervised by the superior. In the literature on organizations, this number is referred to as the span of management or the manager's span of control. It is generally assumed that the smaller is this number, the tighter will be the control exercised by the superior; the larger the number, the looser the control. Unfortunately, there is no way to predetermine what the correct number should be. Estimates in books of organizational principles often suggest ranges, such as 5–8 or 5–14, but Joan Woodward's studies in England[4] revealed successful spans of control as large as fifty while there are many other examples of failures when there has been only one subordinate.

In the 1960s, Harold Koontz devised a contingency model, suggesting that the proper number was a function of several factors or variables, each of which could be assigned a range and a weighting.[5] The model was used by Lockheed Missiles and Space Company who identified their relevant variables as: (1) similarity of functions; (2) geographic contiguity; (3) complexity of functions; (4) direction and control; (5) coordination; and (6) planning. Numbers were introduced in order to make the scheme seem objective, but in reality, both the ranges and the weightings were arbitrary. For example, factors #3, #5, and #6 were weighted as being twice as important as either factor #1 or #2, while factor #4 was considered to be three times as important. The explanation of the reason for this was merely that Lockheed management felt that it represented their situation. As well, it was left to the user of the model to decide where on the range a particular situation should be placed according to how the user interpreted such distinctions as 'simple, repetitive' versus 'routine,' or 'limited supervision' versus 'moderate periodic supervision.' How likely are two observers to agree on the distinction between these pairs? Subjectivity still outweighed objectivity. Furthermore, even if one did work through the exercise, one was not presented with a number to properly describe one's situation, but only a range of numbers whose extremities just happened to approximate the old estimates of 4–11. A proper span of control remains a chimera.

This is not to say, however, that the span of control is unimportant to the organization. Since hierarchy dictates that superiors are supervising somebody, there is a very logical consequence resulting from whatever number of somebodies is decided upon. The proper number may be indeterminate, but some number there shall be. In turn, this number will have a direct effect on the number of levels in the hierarchy, and that produces the dilemma.

There is an inverse relationship between the number of levels in the organization and the span of control. The larger is the span of control, the fewer the number of hierarchical levels required; the smaller the span of control, the greater must be the number of levels. Not every level must have the same span of control, nor even must the superiors on any one level. However, if 600 workers are required to produce the product, it makes quite a difference if a foreman can adequately supervise twenty of them or only five (see Figure 3.2). In the former case, thirty foremen will be required and this number will necessitate at least another two managers on a third level, and finally a fourth level consisting of the chief. In the situation of the span of control of five, there will be 120 foremen for the workers. If in turn, these foremen can only be supervised in clusters of six, twenty more superiors will be required for the third level. These twenty will then require three or four managers on the fourth level. This in turn means that the chief is now on the fifth level and just that much more removed from the workplace.

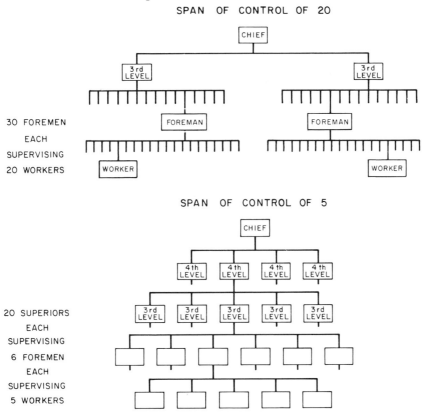

Figure 3.2 Variations in the span of control

And that is the nub of the dilemma. Small spans of control may appear to tighten control for the superior-subordinate relationship, but they loosen the overall control of the organization by extending the number of levels and thereby making the top that much more removed from the bottom. To cut down on the number of levels will reduce the distance between top and bottom, but the resulting increase in the span of control at each level will lessen the control that each level can maintain. What, then, is achieved by eliminating levels in the hierarchy?

Furthermore, it is a well-known phenomenon in organizations that each hierarchical level acts as both a buffer and a screen to the level above it. The buffer may or may not be desired depending upon how close to 'the firing line' top management wants to be. But the screen, which can dilute and standardize communications and render them relatively innocuous, is rarely if ever desired. In eliminating the screens through eliminating hierarchical levels, top management has to increase the span of control of the remaining levels and thereby lessen its control over the subordinates. Which answer does the top management choose?

One approach to resolving this quandary is by setting the span of control at whatever number one can adequately control plus three. That is, if one can control five subordinates, one should have eight of them. Why? Because then one cannot control them. This approach obviously comes down on the side of few levels and less control; however, it is not obvious that that is always the correct side.

For example, research units are notorious for having only two hierarchical levels, the director and the researcher, and a large span of control as a consequence. Control by the director is loose as the researchers examine the problems of the organization according to their own inclinations. The belief is expressed that innovation and creativity cannot be forced, and this belief is often used as a justification in the management of other professionals as well. But are these researchers, or these professionals, actually producing anything worthwhile? It may well be that a smaller span of control, which can ensure that the researchers are focussing on specific problems, will improve the productivity of the unit. In turn, this will lead to an additional hierarchical level and cause the director to be more removed from the researchers. However, if the productivity of the researchers improves, the extra level would be worth this cost.

On the other hand, if the director does not ensure that each superior is keeping his or her span of researchers concentrating on their specific problems, all that will be achieved is an increase in costs for the whole unit. There will be no tighter control than before, and it may even be that the superiors have the researchers examining the favourite problems of the superiors rather than those of the organization. However, if the director does ensure that control is tightened throughout the unit, will this stifle creativity and innovation? Will innovative solutions not be examined because the tighter control procedures do not permit them or reward them? The director now has more control over the unit, but even less contact than before with the individual researchers.

Because of the direct inverse relationships in this dilemma, there is no general solution that can be proposed. Each situation must be looked at by itself and each organization must establish its span of control or its number of hierarchical levels on its own. The only thing that the organization can receive from other organizations or from advisors is the sympathy that comes from their having faced the dilemma themselves. Whether the organization attacks the dilemma from the number of hierarchical levels needed or from the span of control desired, the other half of the dilemma results as night follows day. Ultimately, the resolution will come from trial-and-error and from the satisfaction that results whenever one resigns oneself to living with the consequences of one's decisions.

d. Unity of Command

The essence of a hierarchical organization is that each employee reports to one and only one superior, and takes orders from only that person. The hierarchy is a chain of command that links groups of workers to the level above through a single person. The insistence upon the single superior as being the only issuer of orders is referred to as unity of command. The desired result of this unity of command is that workers will never receive conflicting demands from two or more sources. Unity of command is the modern adaptation of the Biblical statement: 'no man can serve two masters.'

However, there are others who would say, 'lucky is he who has only two masters.' The modern employee receives orders from the superior at work, from both the local and national governments, from wife or husband, from children, from religious ministers, from sports clubs, unions, and voluntary organizations, and from a host of others. Most of these would deny that they are issuing orders, but they cannot deny that they are making demands which often conflict. What is referred to as apathy in our modern industrialized society may be just an attempt by a worker to deny the validity of any or all of these claims.

Even if we restrict our discussion to the workplace, it is highly unlikely that unity of command will be maintained in practice as much as it is upheld in theory. Hierarchy promotes not only specialization amongst workers, but also amongst managers. If the managers are specializing, then it is only natural that each worker will be required to accept orders from different managers about particular facets of the work. Indeed, Frederick W. Taylor promoted this concept as 'functional foremanship,' and stated that each worker should have eight foremen — a route clerk, an instruction card clerk, a cost and time clerk, a gang boss, a speed boss, an inspector, a repair boss, and a shop disciplinarian.[6] However, without even investigating a workplace, this listing suggests that conflicts will arise in Taylor's scheme, between the speed boss and the inspector, for example, or between the instruction card clerk, who has planned each job to the last detail but without a worker present, and the shop disciplinarian whose discretion at the job site rules the worker and the manner of operation.

There is no question that the concept of unity of command serves a useful purpose. The dilemma is that, in preserving order, cohesion, and control through unity of command, the organization may well miss out on the introduction of new ideas, the speedy adaptation to changing problems and situations, and the increased morale that results from group consultation and decision-making. After all, these latter goals are what outside managers and specialists in other parts of the organization, staff personnel for example, are there to achieve. To insist upon unity of command may result in a stodgy, unchanging work situation that becomes gradually less relevant.

On the other hand, without unity of command, whose directive is the employee to follow? What priority should be given to whom? How can there be the stability necessary to promote productivity when the employee is receiving commands from several organizational superiors? How can a schedule be maintained if any superior has the authority to overrule it though confronting the worker with a demand to undertake a different task or a task for a different unit?

It is often suggested that the resolution of this dilemma must result from redefining the principle. That is, instead of 'each employee should have only one superior,' the principle becomes 'each employee should have only one superior for each facet of the job.' By this redefinition, the line superior, the staff accountant, the personnel director, the company lawyer, or any other specialist within the organization can issue directives to the worker concerning that particular speciality for which each is responsible. The redefinition assumes that the boundaries between specialities are distinct and understood, and that any conflicts in demand for the worker's time have been resolved through a list of priorities.

In practice, these assumptions are rarely correct. There are obvious conflicts between a superior's order that furniture, for example, be made to a certain quality and an accountant's demand that workmanship be reduced in order to save money during a period of reduced cash flow. There are also more subtle conflicts arising from interpretations, such as between a personnel director's insistence that a particular assessment form be completed by the employee and the superior together, and the superior's insistence that the form be completed with minimal assistance from the employee. To resolve the dilemma from this redefinition approach, boundaries must not only be distinct and understood, but accepted.

However, many organizational theorists have been concerned that, if unity of command is maintained in its original, rigid form, the organization will not be able to respond with speed to a changing situation. Horizontal communication and directives between hierarchical units is often required to adapt to the changing situation, but this can hardly be achieved quickly if employees must follow the vertical chain of command rather than going directly to the other unit. Henri Fayol suggested that this could be overcome by introducing a 'gangplank principle.'[7] The result would be that each employee can communicate directly with the other unit as long as the immediate superiors are informed of what is happening. The dilemma here is between speed and control; the gangplank principle places speed as the top priority and control by the superior as secondary. It is a valid resolution of the dilemma if communication is all that is involved, but Fayol neglects to state what should happen if it is necessary for the one employee to give a directive to the horizontal counterpart. This directive may well countermand the superior's orders to that employee.

For example, two senior auditors, E and F, are overseeing audits in two differents metropolitan locations (see Figure 3.3). Auditor F decides that she requires an extra junior auditor. Since none are available at the main ofice, she contacts her counterpart, Auditor E, and requests that one of his juniors be loaned to her for several days. She also informs Partner C in the firm, her immediate superior. The 'gangplank' is in operation. However, when her counterpart, Auditor

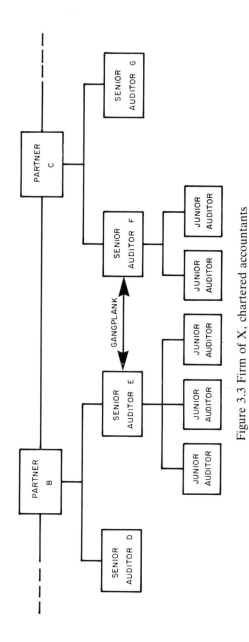

Figure 3.3 Firm of X, chartered accountants

E, informs his supervising partner, Partner B, this partner refuses to allow the junior auditor to be released, citing time pressures as the reason. As well, Partner B stomps down the hall of the main office and demands to know from Partner C what is going on. 'Who is this senior auditor that thinks her work is so important that she can pull workers from my area?' The gangplank is in operation – and now someone has to walk it.

The above example may be trivial, but it is not foolish. Similar situations arise daily throughout the organizational world. Hierarchy creates a dilemma between the desired goal of control and the equally desirable goal of speed. There are no easy answers for resolving the dilemma.

In general, one can suggest that the unity of command should be preserved. That is, each employee must report to and take directives from one and only one superior, no matter what the area of concern. This is the only way that allows the superiors to be aware of what is happening within their units and what resources are available to do what at any given moment in time. If they are to be accountable for the authority that has been assigned to them, then they must have knowledge and control of their resources at all times. If the superiors are willing to be circumvented in certain matters and permit others to give orders directly to their workers, that is their prerogative. However, one can only wish them well and trust that they will remain calm when the crisis arises.

e. Mechanisms for Coordination

The final structural dilemma to be considered arises from the ironic situation that is contained in all hierarchical organizations. These organizations are designed to thrive upon the division of labour. That is, each employee is asked to specialize in one or a few tasks and leave the rest of the required tasks to others. It is generally assumed that specialization or the division of labour will enhance productivity within the organization. The irony of hierarchical organizations is that, having gone to the trouble of making everyone specialize, the organization must then go to more trouble to develop some means or mechanism to coordinate all these specialities. Once again, however, the solution to the problem is not to stop specializing, just as it was no solution to do away with hierarchy because it created problems.

Specialization produces problems, but it also produces benefits whose importance outweighs the inconvenience of the problems. One must overcome specialization problems through mechanisms for coordination, not through eliminating specialities.

Like the word, centralization, coordination is an overworked term. Just as centralization can refer to several disparate concepts, so, too, can coordination. Instead of using the word, coordination, we would be understood more easily if we substituted the actual concept that we are trying to describe — rationalization, standardization, or priorization. These three concepts are not mutually exclusive, but they do describe three distinct organizational needs, all subsumed under the vague term, coordination.

Rationalization refers to the elimination of duplication between two organizational units. As the units develop their specialities, their growth may lead them to overlap. This occurs because, as will be demonstrated in the next chapter, the basis of any specialization is an arbitrary division of the required tasks. Thus, in pursuing the accomplishment of the tasks, units may come to duplicate some of their duties and resources. Rationalization attempts to overcome this and keep each unit to its specific assignment. Each unit will then make its proper contribution to the whole.

Standardization deals with equity. Administrative practices and procedures are made equal throughout the organization so that the treatment of each employee is fair and just. The intent in this type of coordination is not to stress the differences among the units, or their specialities, but to stress their similarities. In that sense, standardization is in opposition to rationalization. Standardization is most evident in financial reporting and personnel matters, but can be found in other areas, too, such as advertising practices. Whereas organizations differentiate roles so as to take advantage of the division of labour, they attempt to treat equitably the people who occupy those roles, and this coordination is standardization.

Priorization is a type of coordination usually imposed on the units of the organization by top management. By priorization is meant a process in which the present and proposed programs of the organization are examined and decisions made as to which ones to pursue now, which ones to pursue in the future, and which ones to reject. Priorization is necessary because no organization has an unlimited supply of resources — men, money, or matériel. Therefore, decisions have to be made within the organization as to what tasks each unit should pursue now and in the future. This type of coordination may remove duplication, but that is not its primary intent. Indeed, it may well create some duplication if the organization attempts to decide which of two processes to use in the future by experimenting in the present with parallel systems or procedures. The purpose of priorization is to prejudge the potential merits of the organization's programs; any other purpose achieved through priorization is secondary.

The dilemma for the organization arises because each of these types of coordination is achieved most logically by a different mechanism. The mechanisms then overlap because their areas of concern are arbitrary. For example, should the hiring of three new engineers to enlarge a program be a responsibility of the program's superior as rationalization of the unit's manpower, a responsibility of the personnel department as standardization of all the personnel of the firm, or a responsibility of top management as a result of their priorization of this program and their need to evaluate their priorities? Whichever mechanism is chosen will be an arbitrary judgement.

As the above example and question suggest, the most logical mechanism for rationalization is the superior who has the responsibility and authority for overseeing the units that need rationalizing. This person will not necessarily be in the top levels of management, but as close to the units as possible, a line manager. The chief duty of the person will be to rationalize the resources of the units and ensure that their contributions mesh successfully with the objectives of the organization.

However, as the example and question also suggest, that person will not be in a good position to standardize all of the practices, procedures, and policies of the organization. To be handled most logically, standardization requires either the perspective of top management or the perspective of a staff unit. In practice, the latter situation is more likely to be adopted by the organization as top management reserves to itself more contentious issues.

Priorization, however, is one of these contentious issues and top management is thus the most logical mechanism to handle it. A staff unit should not have the necessary authority to make line units adhere to its program priorities and the lower-level superior is simply out of the question.

The overall result is that we find each type of coordination handled most logically by a different mechanism and not one of those three mechanisms can adequately handle the other two types. That is, the hierarchical organization has a need for all three mechanisms simultaneously.

We return, then, to the example of who should be responsible for hiring the three new engineers in order to enlarge the program. If top management does not do the hiring, how can they ensure that the most qualified people will be hired to reflect their priorities? If the lower-level superior does not do the hiring, how can that person be assured that these three engineers will both fit well with the unit and not duplicate present resources? If the staff personnel unit does not do the hiring, how can it be assured that the contracts of the three engineers are in line with those in other units, are within the unit's budget, and have been transacted in accordance with the personnel policies of the organization? As in any dilemma, there is more than one objective that the organization is trying to achieve. Unfortunately for the attempts to coordinate, each objective has been assigned to a different part of the organization. Simultaneous achievement of all three objectives is next to impossible in the real world.

In the particular example discussed above, a messy resolution is possible by having representatives of all three mechanisms involved in the hiring. However, in the reality of a busy and complex organization, this is not practical. Instead, the responsibility will be assigned to one of the three mechanisms and the representatives of the other two mechanisms must trust and hope that their requirements will be met. In hiring new employees, perhaps they will.

On the other hand, it is just as likely to suspect that their requirements will not be met and the responsibility will be passed over and over again from the representatives of one mechanism to the next. Standardization can be achieved by the personnel unit, but not rationalization. When dismay is felt that the latter goal is not being achieved, the responsibility will be re-assigned, to the line manager. In time, top management will be bothered because priorization cannot be done, so they will take over the responsibility from the line manager. Both the latter and the personnel unit will now become dissatisfied. Resolution of the dilemma through domination is the only possibility, but it leads inevitably to a transfer of the responsibility as the neglected goal achieves prominence and the achieved goal is taken for granted.

There are a variety of situations within hierarchical organizations that call for the several types of coordination to be achieved simultaneously — for example, the training of future executives; the preparation of annual budgets; the demands made upon researchers or computer facilities; advertising for new personnel — but only the domination of one mechanism will be logical. The benefits to be gained from specialization thus have a consequent cost — coordination. Coordination, itself, has three facets, all equally desirable but not all equally obtainable, and so the organizational decision-makers will have to solve this dilemma perennially.

Notes

1. Herbert A. Simon, *The Shape of Automation for Men and Management*, Harper Torchbacks (New York: Harper & Row, 1966), pp. 99–102.
2. Frederick C. Thayer, *An End to Hierarchy! An End to Competition!* (New York: New Viewpoints, 1973).
3. Robert Michels, *Political Parties*, trans. by Eden and Cedar Paul (Glencoe, Ill.: The Free Press, 1949).
4. Joan Woodward, *Industrial Organization: Theory and Practice* (London: Oxford University Press, 1965), p. 69.
5. Harold Koontz and Cyril O'Donnell, *Management: A Systems and Contingency Analysis of Managerial Functions* (6th ed.; New York: McGraw-Hill, 1976), pp. 293–96.
6. Frederick Winslow Taylor, 'Shop Management,' in *Scientific Management* (New York: Harper & Row, 1947), pp. 100–104.
7. Henri Fayol, *General and Industrial Management*, trans. by Constance Storrs (London: Sir Isaac Pitman & Sons, 1949), p. 35.

CHAPTER 4

Managerial dilemmas

Management should always be thought of as a dynamic process. In fact, managers and administrators would be well advised to think always of themselves as manag**ing** or administer**ing** — an on-going process, never a completed one. Management is a continuous process, not a static occupation. The managing of any operation only ends with the termination of the operation. No manager can ever afford the luxury of thinking that, because the structure of the operation is in place, there is nothing more to do but to sit back and watch it operate.

Therefore, overcoming or resolving the structural dilemmas as listed in the last chapter is not a sufficient conclusion for the manager. Even if those structural dilemmas are resolved to everyone's satisfaction, the manager can be sure that other dilemmas will arise from the dynamic situations that they enfold. The world has both static and dynamic elements. To indicate this split between the static and the dynamic, dilemmas arising from the latter are referred to here as 'managerial dilemmas.' This is not to suggest that managers are not responsible for resolving the structural dilemmas; it is only to clarify the idea that management is a dynamic process and that these particular dilemmas arise from what are commonly referred to as 'the functions of management.'

Accordingly, this chapter has been organized on the basis of these 'functions of management.' There is no standard and well-accepted list of these functions, yet it is a rare management text, especially at the introductory level, that does not refer to them. The original formulation of them is attributed usually to Henry Fayol. A later compilation of them within an acronym, POSDCORB (planning, organizing, staffing, directing, coordinating, reporting, budgeting), is often used as a shorthand reference for them. Any listing of them will contain at least planning, organizing, and controlling as the minimum three.

Nowadays, many writers would disparage the use of these 'functions of management' as being an old-fashioned or out-dated approach to studying management. Yet, as a cursory examination of the books of these same writers would quickly reveal, they spend the first few chapters of their books espousing supposedly-modern approaches, such as contingency theory[1] or a systems model[2] or organizational behaviour,[3] only to fall back on the 'functions' approach for their remaining chapters. The reason for this is that no other approach combines so successfully the sense of dynamism in management with the analytic potential contained in a function-by-function approach.

For example, the more holistic, systems approach may seem to create a more valid representation of the complex, ever-changing reality of an organization in this world, but an analyst cannot deal with all the parts of this reality simultaneously. If one were describing truly a dynamic, complex system, by the time one got to the bottom of the first page, what one had written at the top of the page would no longer be valid. Thus, the analyst looks at individual parts one-by-one, holding the other parts constant for the moment. There is no question that this approach has its faults, limitations, and weaknesses, but it is the essence of the scientific method that has been used to create our industrialized nations. It has obviously great benefits as well as costs.

A more valid criticism of the 'functions of management' approach is contained in the following:

For in his day-to-day administrative activities, the manager does not say to himself that he is planning, that he is ready to commence organizing or directing, or that he is going to stop organizing and begin controlling: he simply makes decisions. He may make planning decisions, organizing decisions, directing decisions, and controlling decisions, yet he may not think of these decisions in terms of these functional areas, and whether or not he does will not alter the fact that what he does as a manager is make choices.[4]

One cannot argue against the proposition that the essence of management is to make decisions. Indeed, a book devoted to the resolution of dilemmas would appear ridiculous if its author so tried. Yet, one can contend that management decisions are not made in a vacuum; they are made with respect to particular functional needs within the organization, such as the need for planning, for organizing, and so on. In fact, Morell concurs with this in the last sentence quoted above. Therefore, a function-by-function approach is not out-of-place if the approach concentrates on the decisions that have to be made within the functional areas. This is the theme of this chapter.

However, it must always be remembered that the naming of functions is solely an artificial device to aid the analyst. What is the distinction between a planning decision and a controlling decision? Is not a plan an attempt to control? Or what is the distinction between an organizing decision and a staffing one? Should the one be made in isolation of the other? Does it make sense to alter the organization without regard to the staff one has, or to staff the organization without regard to the positions one has organized?

It is the artificiality of the functional distinctions, the 'ceteris paribus' mode of analysis, that the holistic approaches attempt to surmount. One must be sympathetic to these attempts because the artificiality of the analyst's classifications has only the most meager of defenses — pragmatism. That is, the artificial constructs appear to allow greater knowledge and understanding to be developed since the dynamics of the totality are beyond simultaneous comprehension. It may seem artificial to divorce an organizing decision from the staff who will occupy these positions; however, if one does not make the separation, if one does not hold the staff equal or constant while designing the structure, then no hypotheses can be tested, no regularities observed, and no principles established. The result of this would be that each situation in the world would have to be considered to be unique or *sui generis*, and there would be no purpose in trying to create a study of management. That is not the scientific approach that has so changed our industrialized societies. For better or for worse, we have appeared to advance through the use of analytic techniques, even if we must always keep in mind that a synthesis of these analytic results is necessary, especially for managing, in order to attempt to cope with the complex, ever-changing reality. In terms of the material in this book, it means that the resolution of a dilemma in one functional area may create a dilemma in another area. That phenomenon was apparent in Chapter Two and will become more apparent in this chapter.

a. Planning

In order to describe managerial practices, Herbert Simon once rewrote Gresham's Law as, 'programmed activity tends to drive out non-programmed activity.'⁵ Programmed activity, or programmed decisions, can be defined as routine, everyday, commonplace decisions that arise constantly in the typical organization. They result from the adjustments that have to be made regularly to accommodate standardized procedures to the individual client, customer, or employee whose situations or circumstances do not quite fit the rule laid down by the procedure.

Non-programmed decisions are the unique, often once-in-a-lifetime, extraordinary decisions that are far more important to the success of the organization than are the programmed ones, but which arise only infrequently. Simon suggests that the combination of their overwhelming importance and their infrequent occurrence tend to cause managers to put them aside until 'tomorrow,' until a less hectic moment can be found in which to contemplate them calmly. Of course, because programmed decisions arise daily and have to be resolved immediately, tomorrow never comes, and the rewrite of Gresham's Law is fulfilled.

These definitions of programmed and non-programmed decisions actually designate the two ends of a spectrum of possible decisions. The vast majority of organizational decisions fall somewhere between these end-points. That is, if the decision is truly routine, it has arisen before and the organization will have established procedures to handle each of the possible alternatives. In these situations, it is probable that any subordinate, or even a computer, can make the decision without involving the manager.

At the other end of the spectrum, if a non-programmed decision is so unique that it has no precedents, no similarities with possibly analogous situations, then it is difficult to envision how a decision can be made by humans short of throwing a dart at a board full of alternatives. And even then, how were these alternatives derived?

Thus, we are left with a variety of organizational decisions falling somewhere along the spectrum of possibilities between programmed and non-programmed. In addition, according to Simon, those that lie toward the programmed end of the spectrum tend to be given priority over those on the non-programmed side.

Planning decisions, unfortunately, fall on the non-programmed side of the spectrum. While everyone recognizes the importance of planning, it tends to be set aside in the flurry of everyday activity that characterizes most organizations. A common organizational expression to describe this phenomenon is: How can we figure out how to drain the swamp when we are up to our knees in alligators! Simon's observation is very appropriate to the planning function.

As a result, many organizations try to overcome the problem by establishing a separate planning unit. This unit may take one of many forms — an office at the vice-presidential level, a staff department or branch, a full hierarchy with counterparts at every level of the line, some combinations of these, or even a different form. No matter which form is chosen, its essence will be to take away the planning function from the activities of the line manager. Since the organization has determined that the line manager has too many programmed decisions to make and has not been carrying out the planning function, this non-programmed function is assigned to a staff planning unit and the line manager is left with the other functions, the more pro- grammed ones.

As soon as this separation of the planning function is achieved, some of the line-staff dilemmas discussed previously in Chapter Three are created. The staff planning unit can concentrate exclusively on preparing plans so that these non-programmed decisions will be made, but what authority does the staff unit have to ensure that the plans are implemented by the line? Furthermore, being separated from the line, how does the planning unit obtain an accurate assessment of the capacities and capabilities of the line such that the plans will be realistic and within the realm of possibility for the line? Finally, the line may actually want to implement the plan and have the resources to do it, but how does it ensure that the staff unit produces the plan by the time it is needed? The staff may not be able to control the line, but can the line control the staff any better? If the plan for the next phase of the work is not created in time, is the line manager to sit idly, marking time, or lay off workers, or go ahead with his or her own interpretation of what needs to be done and ignore the plan when it does arrive?

A typical example of the planning dilemma occurred in the De- partment of External Affairs (DEA) of the Government of Canada during the 1970s. The DEA was asked by the Cabinet to prepare a short list of Canada's foreign policy priorities. The assignment was given to the Policy Analysis Group (PAG) of the department. The PAG, as a staff body, went beyond the original request and prepared a comprehensive set of objectives, as well as a set of measures for the DEA that would allow both for future studies of countries important to Canada and for studies of important issue-areas, such as energy.

However, '. . . PAG's objectives had no significant practical effect, and not a single study employing the format was ever done.'

The reasons given for this lack of action are the classic complaints by line managers: the objectives were too general; decisions had to be made too quickly to allow time for inclusion of the PAG work; the line managers were responsible to their superiors, not PAG; PAG was not aware of the actual problems at the operational level; PAG was perceived as a group of meddlers; the line contended that it was already conducting studies of important problems; line objectives evolve from their daily work and cannot be foreseen meaningfully by outsiders.[6]

The dilemma in planning revolves around who is to do the planning. If each manager is to do his or her own planning, there is a tendency for it not to be done, or not done for very far into the future, or not done comprehensively enough to mesh with the plans of others. To overcome these tendencies, a separate planning unit can be created. However, this does not necessarily resolve all problems because now the tendency is to have plans for the organization that will not, or cannot, be implemented by the line, or are not done in time, or are so comprehensive that they are overly abstract. The parts mesh well on the plan, but can each part understand what it alone is supposed to do?

Libraries are filled with examples of elaborate plans, created by special planning units, that have never been implemented. The government sector is notorious for this phenomenon, but one can find examples in the business sector, too. For example, top management in a travel agency planned to have the agents do more commercial business with firms and less business with private individuals. However, the agents had developed so many contacts with individuals that they had little time or desire to cultivate relationships with businesses. Top management eventually hired a new set of employees to handle only commercial business. What is required in any organization is an assurance that not only will planning be undertaken, but that it will be implemented.

To resolve this dilemma, neither domination nor compromise can be the underlying strategies. This is one of the few examples where Follett's call for integration has a place. The dilemma revolves around the best means for getting the planning done and implemented. Nobody is opposed to the goal of planning, itself.

Domination, such as only the line or only the staff undertaking the planning, has been seen time and again to be ineffectual to resolve the dilemma. In the former case, the line never gets around to the planning function; in the latter, the plan is perceived by the line as an imposition and so its implementation is resisted.

Compromise, too, is rarely effective as a strategy to resolve the dilemma. The compromise usually takes the form of a plethora of committee meetings between various members of the line and staff departments. To many of these members, the number of meetings that appear necessary are not only an infringement on their time, but are hardly productive. The line members want just to be left alone to get on with their work while the staff consider the line to be 'reactionaries,' always objecting to the staff's ideas. The net result of the compromise is that either the line co-opts the staff so that little innovation or commitment ensues, or else the staff ignore the line and work away in an 'ivory tower.' Compromise in this dilemma rarely finds the Golden Mean.

Integration for this dilemma, however, requires an act of faith by both the staff and top management. Integration in this dilemma means that the organization does require a separate planning unit, but it is not the purpose of that unit to plan. If the organization can accept the reasoning behind that paradox, it is well on its way to achieving a successful planning function by its members.

This integrative resolution says that it is not the purpose of the planning unit to plan; the purpose of the planning unit is to ensure that planning is done throughout the organization. There is quite a difference. In this proposal, there are three tasks for the planning unit: (1) to help top-level managers to define the goals and policies for the total organization, or any functional part of it; (2) to coordinate the various plans made by different parts of the organization, but only to ensure that they interlock; and (3) to teach line managers at all levels of the organization how they should go about making their plans.[7] Under this proposal, the staff unit for planning has an educational role only, not an action nor a control role.

The act of faith is required in this role because it will be extremely difficult for either top-level management or the planning unit to evaluate directly the latter's contributions to the organization. The credit for successful action in this world goes to those who act, not those who taught the person how to act. It is no different in this situation. Credit for plans which prove successful will go not to the planning unit, but to those, at whatever level of the organization, who made the plans. There may well come a time in the organization when a series of successful plans made by the line will even cause top-level management to query the very necessity of that appendage, the staff unit for planning.

To maintain success, top-level management must resist that impulse. The work of the planning unit may be 'behind the scenes,' but it is still vitally necessary. In carrying out those three tasks, it is the planning unit that will make the organization knowledgeable about its ever-changing environment, that will take the macro-view to unite the organization into a cohesive entity, that will keep abreast of turnover in management by ensuring that each new manager has the knowledge and skills to perform his or her functions, both programmed **and** non-programmed ones. A planning unit that can perform its role in this manner, as an educator rather than a doer, is more than worth whatever it costs. There may well be other dilemmas in the organization, but there will not be a planning dilemma.

b. Organizing

It would seem strange, in a book devoted to organizational dilemmas, to have a separate and distinct 'organizing' dilemma. Were not the dilemmas associated with headquarters-field operations, with common services, and with span of control, for example, all 'organizing' dilemmas? They were. However, they all had other more important facets as well which demanded that they be catalogued elsewhere. The two 'organizing' dilemmas that are to be considered here have no more logical location.

The principal dilemma in organizing concerns the question — what is the proper basis for organizing? That is, what should be the basis upon which units should specialize? How should departments be differentiated so as to achieve the goals of the organization? Is there a rationale that would support a logical approach to organization?

The classic answer to these questions has been — by one of the four P's. That is, units should be organized on the basis of: (1) purposes (or goals); (2) processes (means or technical specialities); (3) people (or clientele); or (4) place (or geographical location).[8] There are other possible categories as well, such as a 'systems' division into input, processing, and output units. However, the dilemma is not altered by any of these other approaches, as some rationale is still required to differentiate work within these areas. It is the rationale for making the differentiation that is the heart of the dilemma.

Examples of this organizing dilemma can be found easily. For instance, amongst the United Nations Specialized Agencies, which agency should concern itself with agricultural education, or the training and education of people so that they can be better farmers? A valid answer to this question would be to assign the responsibility to the Food and Agricuture Organization (FAO), whose purpose is to improve agriculture throughout the world. However, an equally valid answer would be to assign the responsibility to the United Nations Educational, Scientific, and Cultural Organization (UNESCO), which focuses part of its work on improving the processes of education. As well, however, an argument could be made that the responsibility should be assigned to the International Labor Organization (ILO), whose function is to improve the lot of workers throughout the world. What is the rationale for organizing agricultural education – purpose, process, or people? As will be examined below in more detail, the dilemma is that agricultural education could be handled by any one of these three agencies. More importantly, whichever one does it will result in agricultural education being approached in a quite different way depending upon the organizational philosophy and practices and the personnel of that agency.

Nor is this just a public sector problem; the dilemma arises in the private sector as well. For example, a canning operation may be organized by process or by purpose. (In the private sector, these are more likely to be called 'by function' and 'by product,' but the dilemma is not altered.) In the functional arrangement (see Figure 4.1), the organization may have departments of production, marketing, finance, and personnel with corresponding sub-departments such as manufacturing, purchasing, advertising, selling, accounting, credit, staffing, and records. Each of these departments and sub-departments will have a company-wide perspective and be expected to operate its function for the benefit of every unit in the organization. Each function will be a speciality and there will be no duplication nor need for rationalization within the cannery. This broad perspective has its merits; however, it also makes it difficult to determine the actual profitability of each product.

To overcome this last problem, the company could adopt a product arrangement (see Figure 4.2), such as departments for canned fruit, canned vegetables, canned fish, and canned meat. Each product area

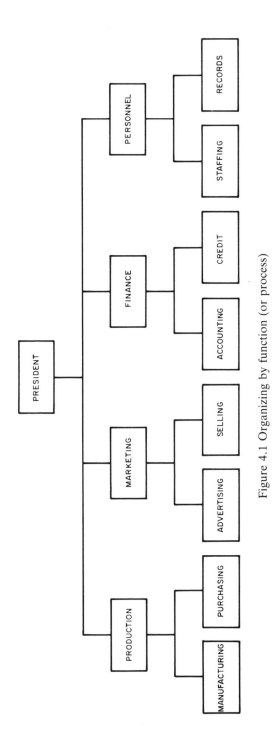

Figure 4.1 Organizing by function (or process)

would be made autonomous and so its contribution to the whole company could be readily ascertained. Top management might now have a better understanding of the merits of each section, but this product method of organizing is not without its faults, too. For example, the independence of each product may lead to a massive duplication of skills throughout the total company — in personnel, in finance, in production, and in marketing. Furthermore, the employees in these areas might be so narrowly specialized that they have quite limited career prospects. As will be shown below, there are other merits and failings associated with each of these two bases that add to the dilemma.

Thus, the basis for organizing is not merely a hair-splitting exercise, such as to determine whether agricultural education is 'a purpose,' 'a process,' or 'a people.' If it were only this, it could be left to the philosophers to resolve. But the basis for organizing is a true dilemma — what are the objectives of the organization and which organizational form will best allow these objectives to be met? The basis that is chosen will have a direct bearing on the quality and quantity of the work accomplished by the organization.

As an illustration of this, the delivery of social work services in an area could either be organized by people (clientele) or by place (geographical area). In the first situation, social workers are specialists: for example, one worker might specialize in problems of the aged; another, in problems of teenage mothers; another, in child abuse; another, with drug addicts; and a fifth, with the unemployed. Each of the social workers has a case file whose people are scattered throughout the geographical jurisdiction of the department.

The main problem with this approach is that many of the cases will reside in the same household. With the situation at its worst, neighbours may one day watch the spectacle of a succession of vehicles arriving from the social work department, each to deal with a different member of the household or even, in some cases, to deal with the same person — that is, the unemployed junkie who vents his frustrations on the baby gotten incestuously from his daughter. Furthermore, even if each of the cases in this particular household is a different person, it is not reasonable to expect that the problems lie solely with the individual person. That is, the social worker dealing with the abused child cannot ignore the unemployed father; the problems of the unwed teenage mother are linked importantly with the other members of the family or household.

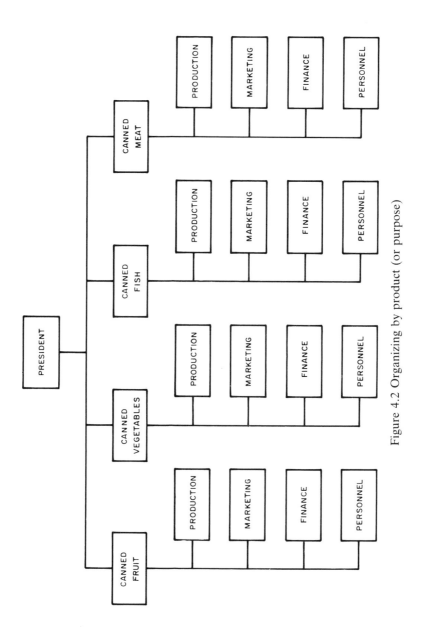

Figure 4.2 Organizing by product (or purpose)

68

Finally, for the social workers themselves, this specialization may make them experts in one area, but is likely to lower their morale through the never-ending succession of similar problems. It may also reduce their career mobility as they do not obtain the opportunity to experience the problems handled by other social workers.

To overcome these three problems of efficiently coordinating the service, of relationships among different caseloads, and of morale, the social work department can be reorganized on a geographical basis, or by place. Now each social worker will be given a caseload containing all the problems within a particular area or territory. Each social worker will become a generalist whose morale should be much higher due to the variety of situations presented and experience gained. Furthermore, the perception of neighbors and other citizens will be that the social work department is efficient and well-organized since there are no 'traffic jams' in front of any households.

But will it be so wonderful within the household? Can this generalist be fully knowledgeable about all the latest research in each one of these problem areas? Can this generalist really do justice to the problems of the aged grandparent, the unemployed father, the drug-addicted mother, the pregnant daughter, and the abused child — or any permutation and combination of these? Furthermore, even if the generalist social worker does have the technical knowledge to cope with all of these different situations, can this person also have the emotional requirements? That is, is it possible for a person to have sympathy for both the abused child and for the unemployed father who vented his frustrations upon the child? If the social worker learns that the teenage daughter got herself pregnant to spite her drug-addicted mother, can one have the requisite sympathy to help them both with their problems? It is more easily written on paper than it is done in practice.

Finally, if the answers to the above are negative, will the morale of the generalist be all that high? Variety may be the spice of life, but one cannot live on spices. Morale is an individual matter. For some people, high morale may result from variety; for others, it may result from a job well-done, even a job that seems monotonous.

The basis for organizing is an important dilemma to be resolved in any organization. Its manner of resolution will determine the attitude and spirit of the employees, amongst other things. The bases may be combined in an organization at different levels (see Figure 4.3), but this does not resolve the dilemma because it will still exist on each level. Furthermore, this will still be an arbitrary action as there is no logical rationale for Purchasing, for example, to be company-wide and Staffing done by each product division (or vice versa). The only manner of resolving the organizing dilemma is the domination of one particular base on any one level, chosen for whatever rationale the organization decides. Of course, as in the discussion of previous dilemmas, this domination may result in a 'reorganization' sometime in the future as the original rationale for the chosen basis is forgotten.

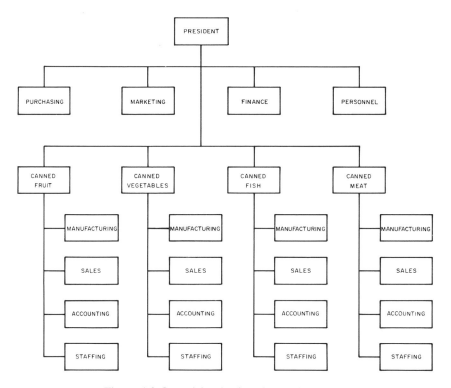

Figure 4.3 Organizing by function and product

In the private sector, such as the cannery, the attempt will probably be to choose the base which is the least-cost solution. Since many costs can be passed on to the customer, a more intelligent approach is to determine what qualities are desired in the business. For example, if it is the profitability of each product that is paramount, then organizing on the basis of product is the answer. However, the company must accept the costs of staff duplication, of narrow, product loyalty rather than company loyalty, and of internal dissension as the products compete with each other. Or it must accept the additional costs of trying to overcome these problems.

If it is the overall control of company activities that is paramount, then organizing on the basis of function or process is the answer. The functional specializations will oversee their activities for the whole firm and the policies and procedures associated with these activities will be standardized throughout. However, this basis may make it very difficult for the accounting section to apportion costs accurately to the various products; it may make the development of top management more difficult as one's functional specialization prevents one from gaining experience in other functional areas; it may lead to neglected products as efforts are spread unevenly throughout the company.

Introducing the bases of 'people' or 'place' will lead to the same points of analysis. For the business to specialize by type of customer or area of the country is a valid perspective, but it will create problems as well as benefits. In effect, to organize by customer or by area is a type of specialization that imitates organizing by product. One merely replaces the products on the chart by a breakdown centered on types of customers (old and young, wholesalers and retailers, or whatever), or centered on areas of the country (east, west, north, south, or whatever).

To get the broader, coordinated perspective of the whole organization, one must organize by function, but that has its limitations, too. The dilemma is such that there is no logical rationale for organizing, whether in the public sector or the private sector. Top management must resolve the dilemma by fiat and the domination of one perspective is the only possible result.

Associated with this organizing dilemma is a further dilemma that arises from any reorganization that is attempted. It was noted that both the social work department and the cannery could be reorganized on a different basis were it to be decided that different objectives were desirable. The reorganizing dilemma occurs because it is not just boxes and words on an organizational chart that are reorganized, but people. Individual human beings are the cause of success or failure of the reorganization, not the organization chart.

This being so, what should be the basis of the reorganization — the capabilities of the present personnel, or the desired structural form? Should one establish the organizational structure first and then find the right people to occupy the positions? Or, should one assess the competencies of the present staff and design an organizational structure to make the best use of them? Either method has its assets and its liabilities.

In the first half of the 1900s, the answer from the organizational theorists would have been to choose the former method — that is, design the structure and then locate the necessary employees. The philosophy behind this was that there is an ideal structure for any situation and one should strive to obtain that ideal. Having determined that ideal structure, then and only then should one hire the people to work within that structure. For example, if one wished to reorganize the social work delivery system from a clientele basis to an area basis, one should do that first and then fit in the present social workers as best as possible. If these social workers could not adapt to the new basis, they could be replaced by others who could. Since people are more adaptable than structures or technology or machines, the classic theorists believed that it was people who should be molded to fit the requirements of the work situation.

For a variety of reasons, some personal, some organizational, later theorists disagreed with the structure-first perspective. They believed that consideration of the qualities and characteristics of human beings should predominate and then one should structure the organization to fit these people. They believed that there was no such thing as an ideal structure for a particular situation and thus there was no merit in pursuing the structure-first approach. Furthermore, even if there were ideal structures for particular situations, there were no ideal people and so one would never locate the required staff anyway. Moreover, it was disgraceful to treat employees as expendable units of production. It was noted in the first organizing dilemma that organizational structures have no absolute basis and it is also known that structures evolve through time and are modified by the people who work within them; therefore, said the later theorists, the people-first perspective should be paramount.

Like so many of the dilemmas, the pendulum has swung back and forth for this one, too. In the 1950s and 1960s, the momentum was behind the people-first perspective. However, the contingency approach to management would now like to swing the pendulum back to the structure-first perspective. Contingency theorists recognize that there may be no ideal organizational structure in general, but they suggest that there are ideal structures for particular situations — if only one can identify the situation one confronts. (This was noted, for example, in the discussion of the span of control dilemma in Chapter 3.) The structure-first perspective would challenge the people-first perspective by asking the question — what happens to the organization when the employees, for whom the accommodating structure was designed, quit or retire or leave the organization for any reason? People are not only adaptable, they are mobile. Where does the people-first perspective find the replacements, or does it require another reorganization?

The only answer to this is a weak one, a rebuttal question that asks the structure-first perspective if there is any merit to designing a structure if one cannot guarantee that there will be the necessary workers and managers to staff it. This suggests that some form of compromise is necessary to resolve the dilemma. However, the domination of either perspective is also possible. Of course, as has been shown, either form of domination may bring weaknesses as well as strengths, but that is not unexpected in organizational situations.

Compromise will be messy. An ideal structure that looks smart and symmetrical will not be possible. There may be inequity as a competent employee may have more duties and responsibilities than a less competent colleague, although both may have the same job title. The compromise reorganization will not work 'according to the book,' but it may well work, at least for awhile.

For example, after a high school system was reorganized so that a small school was closed and its staff and students sent to a larger school, the larger school had 4 secretaries but only enough work for 3½. So one of the secretaries had her work-week divided between that high school and an elementary school which needed an extra half-person. Since this secretary was very competent, the compromise worked well.

However, she left after two years to work for a local business. Her replacement was just as competent, but did not like the split duties and the work of the elementary school was often neglected. As a result, the elementary school succeeded in the next budget in obtaining a new secretary so that it would no longer require the services of the high school secretary. This would have been alright with the high school, except that it now had a competent secretary with not enough work to keep her busy. The compromise resolution is effective, but only so long as the original reorganization and personnel are present.

When reorganizing, if one does not take into consideration the capabilities and desires of the present employees, it is unlikely that the reorganization will succeed. However, if one goes to the other extreme and considers only the needs of these employees, then there is not much point in reorganizing them (assuming that the work is being adequately done at present). A compromise between the two perspectives is required, but it can be chaotic and inequitable, and will most likely be impermanent. It is not surprising that reorganizations follow reorganizations follow reorganizations, whether the cause is to resolve centralization, authority, coordination, or any of the other dilemmas discussed in this book. Resolutions of dilemmas not only lead to constant reorganizations, but the basis of reorganizing is itself a dilemma. Constant problems and new decisions can only be expected as a result.

c. Staffing

The principal dilemma in staffing the organization arises from the potential conflict between long-term objectives and short-term ones. Should the organization develop a 'career staffing system' or a 'job staffing system'? The intent of the former is to hire people whose immediate worth to the organization is not great, but who will be of lasting benefit after the necessary training and development; the intent of the job system is to hire people who have the necessary expertise to help the organization now with much less concern for what will happen in the future.

The characteristics of the career system are thus in direct opposition to those of the job or position system. In the career system, people are hired on, usually at the lowest levels of the organization or at least at the bottom of their career ladder. They are not expected to have any particular expertise at the time, but merely a general education suitable for that ladder. However, they are expected in the long-run to develop the qualities needed to allow them to take successively higher positions in the hierarchy. This means that the organization must undertake to provide them with the necessary training or managerial education that allows them to perform successively more responsible work. As well in the career system, whatever rank or status the employees have at any moment has accrued to them as persons, not because of the particular work they are doing at that moment. That is, their titles, such as second secretary, or senior lecturer, or junior teller, indicate their career advancement, not the particular work they are undertaking. For example, one cannot tell from their titles what work a junior teller does vis-à-vis what a senior teller does, or vice versa. As a result, the generalist training and development of the career system permit the employees to be deployed without loss of status wherever the organization needs them.

In contrast, the job or position system allows people to be hired to fill vacancies wherever they exist in the hierarchy, from top management to the lowest level. These people are expected to have a particular speciality or expertise that allows them to be immediately successful in that position. If they never develop further so that they might be promoted to a higher level in the hierarchy, that is not the concern of the job system. Therefore, whatever status these people have in the organization is a direct result of the particular positions they hold. Rank is in the job.

The ever-increasing specialization in jobs that has characterized the twentieth century, plus the introduction of scientific management concepts into personnel systems,[9] have made the job system the dominant system throughout the Western industrialized world. In fact, it is a rare management textbook that even mentions the career system, much less explains it. In turn, it is a rare organization that has any cognizance of it, even those that use it. This was not always so, and indeed there are still many examples of the career system. Within the public sector, foreign service departments appear to be the last strongholds of the career system as most other departments have fallen before the onslaught of the 'business-efficiency' concepts recommended by such review groups as the Fulton Commission (United Kingdom), the Glassco Commission (Canada), or the Hoover Commissions (United States of America). However, universities, schools, churches, and many charitable organizations have retained the career system, and many organizations in the private sector have as well, suggesting perhaps that the efficiency resulting from job specialization is not necessarily the prime concern of all businesses. Examples of such businesses are: professional firms, such as lawyers, accountants, or engineers; service organizations, such as banks, hospitals, or libraries; and small organizations, such as farms, grocery stores, or tailors. Although the career system does not receive much of a hearing these days, perhaps because personnel administration is itself becoming a specialty in large organizations, the career system is certainly very much in use.

Which system, then, should an organization choose? Can an organization combine the best elements of both?

The career system is criticized for being conservative, overly protective of its employees, for emphasizing seniority over ability, for restricting the input of new ideas and 'fresh blood' to the lowest levels, where they are rarely if ever acknowledged. The criticisms have the validity of all generalizations; they indicate tendencies, but they can be negated by the actions of senior individuals who do have the ability to seek out and introduce new policies and programs into the organization. On the asset side of the ledger, the career system can breed loyalty and commitment to the organization, and can create a high level of either specialist or generalist expertise from a lifetime of either working on or managing the problems of one area.

Of course, loyalty, itself, can introduce another dilemma into the organization. If the employee has too little loyalty or commitment to the organization, one cannot rely on that employee for decisions and judgements that will always benefit the organization. This is the principal fault with the job system.

But the employee could also have so much loyalty that he or she is merely a 'yes-man,' once again of limited use to an organization that needs a critical perspective of its activities. The career system is faulted for creating these 'yes-men' as much as the job system is faulted for leading to the other extreme.

Since neither extreme is desirable, domination is not the answer to this loyalty dilemma. What is wanted is a 'Golden Mean,' a balance or compromise between too much and too little loyalty and between too little and too much criticism. This target is extremely difficult to hit. It will move over time as the circumstances that face the organization change. It will also move as individual employees change, growing older or wiser or both. It will vary from situation to situation depending upon the importance of that situation to the organization. And it will vary for employees' decisions depending upon the recipient of that loyalty — that is, the organization, top management, the immediate supervisor, or some other body.

For example, some secondary school teachers in a rural system were extremely critical of what they considered to be old-fashioned techniques and principles of the headmaster for disciplining students. Although they were all agreed on their disapproval of the headmaster's methods, they could not agree on what means to express their concern, and soon split into three factions.

One faction said that their prime loyalty was to the school system and they should take their criticism to the superintendent and the board, and perhaps even to the public media. The second faction said that their loyalty was to the students and their education, and so they should try to counteract the headmaster within the classroom. The first faction thought this faction was cowardly, and the second thought the first was a bunch of loudmouths and glory-seekers.

The third faction said that they were loyal to all parts of the system, including the headmaster, who, after all, was still an outstanding teacher and administrator even if a poor disciplinarian. They felt that the teachers should try to live with the situation, balancing the bad against the good. They were contemptuous of the first faction for wanting to ignore the hierarchy and involve outsiders and of the second faction for trying to undermine the organization and its authority from within. In turn, the other factions could agree on one matter — that the third faction was a group of timid, weak-kneed yes-men.

Which faction was closest to the target? Which balanced best the opposing goals of loyalty and criticism?

The lack of loyalty is not the only drawback to the job system. Although the job system would appear to bring outside ideas and expertise immediately to the position where they are needed, there is no guarantee that the experience gained in the outside organization will be applicable in the present organization. Does a middle-manager from an automobile manufacturer really understand the techniques, policies, and problems of an electricity utility? Furthermore, to the extent that the employees of the present organization resent the hiring of a person at a level above them, therefore cutting off their career advancement, the new ideas may not be accepted and adopted even if they are applicable. The job system does not encourage internal loyalty, nor commitment to solving the problems of the organization, to be created. It provides no incentive for employees other than that of trying to improve themselves at the expense of other employees. It may result in high morale for all those who move easily from job to job, but it does nothing for the morale of those who are conscientious, or who would prefer a collective approach to problem-solving over an individualistic approach.

The job system has resulted in a new phenomenon, the person who is a 'two-year wonder.' This person spends one year learning about the organization, a second year making crucial decisions, and then moves onward and upward to another organization on the strength of these two years. Meanwhile, back in the first organization, the employees are left in the third year to sort out the consequences of all those decisions that 'wonder-boy' made. The world only hears that X has an important new job in an even more prestigious organization; the world is never told what a mess X has left behind in the old organization.

In effect, what the staffing dilemma is all about is aptitude versus attitude. By aptitude is meant the expertise to accomplish a task, and this is the essence of the job system; by attitude is meant the socialization of the employees to organizational norms, and this is the purpose of the career system. In fact, every organization wants both of these qualities, and the apparent dichotomy is only created because each system stresses the one quality over the other. Every employer wants both aptitude and attitude in the employees. Although domination is a plausible resolution to this dilemma, it makes little sense in reality. Both qualities are desired in one's employees.

An integration to achieve the virtues of both systems would appear to be the most desirable resolution, but it, too, makes little sense in reality. The two systems are at opposite poles. They are both desirable goals, but one system can only be introduced at the expense of the other. The dilemma is not strictly between aptitude and attitude, but between career system and job system. The best resolution that one could obtain would be some form of compromise.

Can the dilemma be resolved through attempting to create a better balance or compromise of the two systems? To a certain extent, it can. For example, within a particular position, such as stenographer, a career can be introduced by having the person work up from Steno 1 to Steno 2 to Steno 3, and so on. Both Steno 1 and Steno 3 are doing the same work, typing correspondence, filing, handling the public, but Steno 3 is recognized by the organization as having more ability and a longer service. Similarly, any other job, such as programmer-analyst, assembly line worker, painter, manager, can be 'numbered' in this manner to reflect both ability and seniority.

However, the compromise resolution will break down if outside people can be hired directly into the upper numbers over the heads of others in that career line. In this case, the organization has decided that the domination of the job system is the paramount policy and no one will be deceived by the career levels. That is the organization's decision to make, but it should not be surprised if the result is low morale, high turnover, and an endless succession of 'two-year won-ders.' Nor should it be surprised if it has difficulty getting the managers of different branches or units to cooperate with each other, to make decisions that coordinate the units, and to sacrifice the resources of the unit for the good of the organization. For better or for worse, the job system is not designed to obtain these results.

Another method of achieving a compromise is to have broader job descriptions within the job system. As a result, the employees would not be expected to be so narrowly specialized that they would have no prospect of rising higher within the organization. They would bring to the job a larger set of capabilities than the job required immediately.

Of course, like any compromise, this one can be abused, too. Job descriptions are often written today for what are technically career positions with the result that the job description is so meaningless as to be ridiculous. This happens especially when top-level managers are desired and the organization has a specialty-oriented personnel de-partment that is imbued with a love of the job system.

For example, the following specifications were made for the job description of a Principal of a Community College:

The College Principal is the chief executive officer . . . and is responsible for its over-all operation in accordance with provincial legislation under policy as set by the College Council. The role of the College Principal requires a person who will give the College positive leadership in interpreting and fulfilling its educational role in the community.[10]

Recognizing that that job description is broad and vague, an attempt was then made to define the job more succinctly through the use of examples of responsibilities and desired qualifications. However, these were scarcely less vague. For example, they included such items as: represent the College; create a favourable climate; serve as the chief public relations officer; communicate personally with, and relate to, the constituent parts of the College; assume ultimate administrative responsibility. Would anyone have expected less, or different?

In effect, the College Principal is the culmination of a career in which one has demonstrated the possession of certain qualities and abilities. However, since the organization has established a job sys-tem, the career positions have been subjected to job descriptions, too. A compromise has resulted such that the job descriptions have form but no substance. Like many another compromise, neither objective is achieved. The organization would be well advised to allow one system to dominate, preferably the career system since job specifications in education are not adapted easily or meaningfully to the requirements of the job system. However, there will be other work situations where the compromise of a broader job description in a job system does have validity.

d. Controlling

In the introduction to this chapter, it was suggested that one could not differentiate validly between, for example, a planning decision and a controlling one. 'Is not all planning an attempt to control?' was the question asked. In fact, one could use this line of reasoning with all the management functions. Is not staffing an attempt to control? Is not organizing an attempt to control? What, then, is a controlling decision that is peculiar to itself?

There are two distinct areas of concern that answer this question, and many sub-areas or variations within them. On the one hand, there is an attitudinal area; on the other hand, a locational area. That is, there are controlling dilemmas that have in common the resulting attitudes of the people being controlled; and there is a control dilemma that arises from the location or position of the control or evaluation mechanism within the organizational structure. The latter could be said to mirror the planning dilemma discussed previously in this chapter. Both attitudinal and locational control dilemmas will be examined in this section.

It should be recognized that the term, 'control,' is being used in as broad a manner as possible. In this definition, control is viewed as the fundamental fact of human existence. Control can be as individualistic as breathing to control the self; it can be a social phenomenon as in shaking hands to control another; and it can be an organizational phenomenon as in issuing orders to guide the workings of groups of people. It is the last with which we are concerned.

It should be noted as well that control is always at least a bilateral process. Both the controller and the controllee are controlled by whatever control process is chosen. This is what gives rise to the attitudinal dilemmas of control. Of course, the control process is not one of reciprocity, even if it is bilateral. The slave driver is controlled by the whip, but he or she certainly does not suffer from the process as do the slaves — at least not physically. However, the slave driver's mental outlook on work, and life in general, is affected by the control process that he or she implements daily, and that is what is meant by the statement that it is a bilateral process. Those who spend their working hours disciplining others are likely to believe that severe discipline is also the solution for family and society situations.

What types of controls, then, should the controller institute? On the one hand, there are what might be called 'external' controls: stop watches, time clocks, sign-in books, and the like. These are negative controls. On the other hand, there are 'internal' controls: a sense of pride or professionalism, a desire and willingness to accept responsibility for one's actions, an ability to measure one's progress against a set of objectives or standards. These are usually referred to as positive controls.

The negative, external controls are denigrated by modern management theorists and the positive, internal controls are extolled as virtuous. The issue is not really so black-and-white.

It may well be true that the external controls do not motivate positively. The employee is not encouraged by them; the employee's only concern is to satisfy the requirements of the control and thereby avoid any punishment. This is why the controls are said to be negative. Minimal compliance is their result. In Chapter Three, the same contention was made for the two bases of authority, positional and personal.

In fact, many employees will make a game out of seeing just how minimally they can comply before the employer takes action. Arriving right on time realizes no punishment. What about one minute late? Two minutes? Three? At what point does the employer 'crack the whip' and insist that the employee obey the rules?

On the other hand, external controls are equitable to all employees. There is no favouritism with them. They are clear and objective and their intent is easily understood. There may be a valid reason why an employee has broken the rule, but there is no doubt in the minds of anyone that the rule is broken.

The opposite conditions exist for internal controls. They are said to motivate employees positively because they are supposed to encourage employees to act responsibly and to undertake even more than what the job requires as a minimum. Initiative and enthusiasm are expected to result from using positive, internal controls.

In practice, however, the organization may not be established in such a manner that the positive motivation has an outlet. With the ever-increasing specialization of employees, there may be no outlets for the enthusiastic employee to show initiative.

For example, one bank encouraged its tellers, when they had 'closed off' for the day and reconciled their transactions, to look around and help others in the bank to finish their day's work. However, if Teller X finished early and offered to help Tellers Y and Z, he was rebuffed because they were responsible personally for shortages and did not want anyone to mix them up halfway through their reconciliation. Nor could Teller X help the Loans Officer, as he had no training in that area; nor the Posting clerks because each worked at a machine; nor the Accountant and Manager as they had their own responsibilities. So Teller X left the bank and walked across the street to luxuriate in the beauty of a swan-filled park. A few minutes before quitting-time, he returned to the bank in order that he could be seen to go home at the same time as everybody else. Was he motivated positively? He was not. After a few days, the park no longer attracted him and he merely dragged out his own reconciliation until quitting-time.

Of course, one could say that Teller X should have been allowed to leave when his work was done. But would that have been equitable to the other tellers? Would they perceive this as a reward, or only the result of X having an easier job because he did not keep his window open as long as they did since he took longer lunch hours and coffee breaks? Or, knowing the tricks of the trade themselves, they might even perceive it as the result of X dawdling over an easy transaction through conversation with a customer because he had noticed that the next person in the queue had a difficult transaction with lots of work and different forms required.

In other words, because the positive controls are self-applied, they can be seen to be inequitable. Unless one has secure, confident employees that can be satisfied with their own individual actions, one may create as many problems as one solves by introducing internal controls.

In the above example of the bank, the manager was told repeatedly by the other employees of the perceived inequity in Teller X's workload. So the manager switched completely to external controls, supervising coffee breaks and lunch hours, insisting that opening and closing times be rigidly observed, and instituting other rules and regulations to maintain discipline. Morale fell amongst the employees as no excuses were accepted, and the manager, himself, became despondent because it seemed that he was spending all his time supervising 'a shiftless bunch.' When Teller X quit, the manager ensured that he replaced him with a slower, less intelligent person, convinced that a banking situation could not operate with positive, internal controls.

The attitudinal dilemma in controlling is one that has to be resolved through the domination of one set of controls over the other. Modern management theorists would suggest that these controls should be always the positive, internal controls, but they can present no proof for this, only case study evidence. Each situation must be examined individually; what works in one place will not necessarily work in another. On the surface, positive, internal controls appear to be better motivators for both employees and the manager, but they may not produce equity, unity amongst the employees, and conformity to the organization's standards. Negative, external controls will achieve these goals, but possibly at the price of dispirited managers and employees who try to get away with doing as little work as possible. In the latter case, if the work is well-defined, as in the bank example, this may not be a problem.

Elsewhere the organizational superiors may well find themselves in the classic dilemma, see-sawing back and forth from one approach to the other as conditions change. If this happens, they would be best advised to choose one approach over the other and accept the ensuing consequences. As a general rule, one can think back to the 'bureaucracy' dilemma of Chapter Three. Where the work is predominantly maintenance-oriented, external controls are probably superior, given the characteristics of the employees that are involved; where the work is adaptive-oriented, internal controls will probably work better as the employees will probably be more highly educated. Again, however, each situation must be examined for its own merits.

The locational dilemma in controlling is of a different quality. Here the problem arises from the need to evaluate a government or business program, or obtain feedback concerning the methods of operation of the line, or judge the worthiness of a service to its clients or customers, or some like thing. This dilemma is simple and straightforward — should the people involved in the activity undertake the measurements, assessments, and evaluation, or should some other people, separate from the activity, undertake these? To a certain extent, it is a special case of the line versus staff dilemma.

If the people involved in the activity undertake these control measures, can an honest assessment be expected? These people, the line, have the most to lose in the event of waste, mistakes, or inefficiencies being discovered. Why should one expect them to adopt assessment procedures that will reveal their inadequacies? Furthermore, even if they are honest, do they have the skills necessary to test and assess operations? Finally, even if they are honest and do have the required skills, are they enough removed from the operation that they can be objective and unbiased rather than subjective? That is, will they subject the operation to a rigid and rigorous scrutiny, or will they merely accept a weak and casual test that reflects well on their work?

To avoid these difficulties, the organization can have a special evaluation unit established. This will be a staff group who will assess each operation objectively and honestly as outsiders, and then direct the line people to implement any necessary corrections or improvements. As specialists, they will use the most rigorous methods, the latest available, and no one will be able to doubt their integrity.

But will the line accept their suggestions? Why should the line implement these corrections or supposed improvements? First of all, what allows these outsiders to even think they understand the operations and all the special circumstances with which the harried line supervisor has to cope? And what makes the outsiders think that their evaluation methods, probably taken from some textbook, are applicable to this particular operation? Finally, even if the line supervisor does accept and implement these supposed improvements, what if they turn out to be not so good after all? Who will bear the brunt at the end of the next review, the staff outsiders (not likely) or the line supervisor who did not really understand what they were recommending? There is little or no incentive for the line in this resolution of the dilemma, even if a better evaluation has been made.

As in the situation of the planning dilemma, the best resolution of this locational control dilemma is once again an integration of the two possibilities. The problem lies not in whether or not to evaluate; no one will deny the merits of an assessment. The problem lies in the means by which to undertake that assessment. Thus, it is not the proper role of the outsiders, the evaluation group, to evaluate. Their proper role is to help the line people evaluate their own operations. They must be teachers and advisors, not active controllers. Their job is to assist the line people to learn the latest and most appropriate methods for measuring performance, the latest advances in assessment, the relation of ends and means for critical evaluation. From this knowledge will come the line's willingness to implement the necessary improvements or corrections. The solution is the same as for the planning dilemma, and has the same pitfalls.

Control cannot be seen as an imposition by others if we want to avoid resistance to it. Therefore, we must integrate to resolve properly this locational dilemma. If we do not care about the resistance, then it does not matter which approach to resolving the dilemma we choose. However, we will then have either a minimal effort by the line in evaluating themselves, or a minimal result because the staff outsiders are ignored. Either one is a waste of everyone's time and effort. In this specific sense, resistance to control, both the attitudinal dilemma and the locational dilemma are related.

e. Budgeting

Because private sector employees are said to be judged by 'the bottom line' (i.e., profits), it is often assumed that budgeting is solely a public sector phenomenon. Nothing could be further from the truth. The vast majority of employees, whether public or private sector, work to a budget. Indeed, the vast majority of financial decisions in all organizations, even those where profits are expected, are made with respect to a budget. Budgets are plans. If the plan is accurate, there may be profits at the end of the time period, but the decisions that result in those profits will be made with regard to a budget.

However, budgets are not just planning devices; they are also controlling devices. It is from this dual purpose that the budgeting dilemma arises. (The locational dilemmas associated with planning and controlling that were discussed previously are applicable also to budgeting, but they will not be repeated here.) The problem is — can the same budget be both a planning device and a controlling device? The terminology and examples to be used in this discussion will be drawn from the public sector, but the dilemma is equally a factor in the private sector.

Historically, budgets have been of the line-item type. This has meant that each item of expenditure (e.g. postage, office equipment, salaries, *et al.*) has occupied a line of the budget, and the total budget is merely an accumulation of all those items and their projected costs.

Those people charged with approving the budget are required to evaluate each item of expenditure and the overall total.

For these people, their principal point of reference is the comparison to be made with the amount that was budgeted and spent for each item in the preceding time period. Any discrepancies between the two time periods must be justified by those who prepared the budget, and the justification is then accepted or rejected by the authorizing body. Most often, those who prepare the budget, such as civil servants, are more familiar with departmental operations and needs than those who approve the budget, such as the politicians, and so the justification is accepted. As well, in both inflationary periods and in times of growth, there is an automatic assumption that more money needs to be budgeted for each item of expenditure in each succeeding time-period.

The faults with the line-item budget are chiefly two. First, it does not say exactly what the department plans to achieve from these expenditures. Secondly, it does not say why this combination of expenditures will best achieve the department's goals.

That is, the line-item budget lists only the means that have been chosen by the department; it gives no indication of the ends that those means are supposed to be achieving, and it gives no assessment of alternative means that might have been chosen. It does not help the politician to know that £X were spent on postage and £Y on long-distance telephone calls if the politician does not know why the department needed to communicate with anybody in the first place.

As a result of these faults, many governments have turned to program budgeting. The essence of this method is that the department begins by indicating its goals or ends and then determines which set of alternative means will best achieve those goals. The budget is then constructed as the package of expenditures necessary to achieve the end or program. The politicians are asked to approve the package or, under a variant called zero-based budgeting, may even be asked to select the final package from an array of alternative packages that includes a zero package (i.e., one that included the effects to be obtained if the program were not to be implemented at all). The program budgeting method should allow the politicians to see exactly what level of benefits the program will produce and exactly what expenditures are required to achieve that level.

Unfortuantely for the good intentions behind program budgeting, in practice it works no better than does line-item budgeting. There are three reasons for this.

The first reason is that the politician is actually at a greater disadvantage under program budgeting than under line-item budgeting. With the former, the politician is presented with a package of expenditures, all supposedly interrelated so that none can be altered. At least with the line-item budget, the politician can use practical knowledge to assess the real likelihood that a particular item, such as postage, needs to be increased so greatly. No such opportunity exists with the program budget. The politician must accept or reject the whole package. Therefore, with this method, the politician is even more at the mercy of the civil servant that the particular package is the optimum combination of expenditures. And because of the uncertainty of the future, that is something which no one can prove.

Which leads to the second reason. How does one determine what are the goals or ends of any program? Is the goal of vocational education, for example, to train technicians for the long-term future, to keep unemployed youth off the streets, to fill manpower shortages in the short-term, to provide mobility to the lower classes, or even something entirely different? Until the end is agreed upon, no package of means is possible, optimum or not. However, it is likely that the politicians have all of these objectives in mind, although they will be reluctant to state them. In any case, whether they do or do not, the goals may be in conflict such that no 'package approach' can achieve them all simultaneously.

Furthermore, the ends or programs of many departments may overlap, such as mentioned in the organizing dilemma with agricultural education. One cannot separate out the agricultural component of the education department and the educational component of the agricultural department in order to construct a program for agricultural education without making arbitrary judgements about overhead costs and what percentage of an employee's time is apportioned to agricultural education vis-à-vis vocational education.

Finally in this area of goals and ends, is it agricultural education, for example, that is the end of the program, or is it something more than that? That is, is the goal to educate farmers, or is the goal something above and beyond that — to increase agricultural productivity? If the latter, it may well be that some other package, such as improved mechanization rather than improved education, may be the optimum alternative. But even increased agricultural productivity may only be a means itself to improved nutrition for the total populace. Which, in turn, may be only a means to better health, and thus the program budget for health improvement is not the optimum package unless it has been constructed in conjunction with that for agricultural education. And one can keep going beyond this. Is better health the goal or is it really a better life for each citizen, and is that a quantitative factor of years alive, or is it a qualitative factor composed of a variety of experiences, or something else? How can a valid budget be constructed that indicates the interrelatedness of programs when the interrelatedness is merely a summation of arbitrary judgements? One might just as well work from the arbitrary increases in a line-item budget where the figures are at least more easily understood.

The qualitative factor leads to the third reason why program budgeting is no better in practice. How does one account for the qualitative factor in programs? Because budgets are quantitative judgements, data must be quantified to be included. The process of quantification, however, is most often an arbitrary judgement as to the quality of the program, or why citizens have chosen the program. For example, how can literacy be measured without an arbitrary judgement as to what constitutes literacy? Is it the ability to write one's name, or balance one's chequebook properly, or read and understand the Bible, or what? Or, can a simple head-count really say why citizens choose a particular form of recreation, such as using a park, such that an optimum package can now be created to foster that recreation? In effect, the program budget attempts to be more exact than the line-item budget, but in fact is no more so.

Ever since Charles Lindblom identified line-item budgeting with 'muddling through,' people have attempted to create a more rational, comprehensive approach to budgeting, such as program budgeting.[11] But what Lindblom was saying was that not only was 'muddling through' the most common method, it *should* be the method chosen. That is, it is not possible in Western industrialized democracies, where parliaments and legislatures are the focal points of compromise, to improve upon the 'muddling through' characteristics and yet allow the politicians to remain in control. It may not even be possible for the politicians to remain in control using line-item budgeting, but at least it is more likely. Line-item budgeting acknowledges that compromises were reached for the last time-period, which therefore allowed the budget to be constructed and implemented. Accordingly, unless there are some radically different demands from the citizenry to alter that set of compromises, the budget for this time-period should merely reflect those compromises, with minor, incremental changes to accommodate inflation and any other routine differences that are required.

For the private sector, the reasoning is no different. The budget in a business is a set of compromises among the various departments. The production department would like to upgrade its equipment during the coming year; the marketing department would like to institute a world-wide advertising campaign and hire more salespeople; the accounting department insists it would be able to keep better control if it had a different computer facility. Each department would like a larger budget and all are quick to show how the increased expenditure will bring an even greater increase in profits. Top management is more realistic, realizing full well that the projected expenditures may be accurate but the projected revenues are only wishes. Their problem is similar to the politicians — should all departments receive authorization for the major increases in spending? Should only some receive the authorization, and which? Or should each department receive an incremental increase over its last budget and therefore retain the set of compromises that worked last time?

The dilemma arises because the program budget is superior as a planning device, but it removes operational control from the authorizing body. The line-item budget, on the other hand, is excellent for control, especially by the authorizing body, but is inferior as a planning device. Neither type of budget is perfect, even for those areas where it excells, because each is only a future projection as to how people will behave and act in other organizations, in one's own organization, and in the world at large.

The solution to the dilemma is to recognize that there are two distinct needs in the organization and to devise two different budgets to attempt to satisfy, and even reconcile, those needs. Overall, however, the line-item budget must be the dominating one. It, alone, allows the authorizing body to exert control over the operations of the organization, and to be held accountable for the compromises that are necessary to allow the several parts of the organization to work and work together. Program budgets, especially when they cut across departmental boundaries, negate accountability both in business and in governments where ministers are held responsible for a particular department.

This solution of choosing the line-item budget may seem conservative as it justifies the *status quo*. It does not have to. New programs and new methods can be introduced by justifying them on their merits and then incorporating them into the line-item budget. Similarly, outdated measures can be eliminated if everyone agrees to do it. Both of these aspects are not pertinent to the dilemma. What is pertinent is to decide whether a purported rational, comprehensive, planning approach to budgeting is more important to the organization than an incremental, compromising, accountable control approach — and the answer is no.

f. Directing

In one sense, the process of directing can be said to be like that of controlling. It pervades everything that a manager does. In that sense, many 'directing' dilemmas have already been discussed, such as 'unity of command,' 'centralization versus decentralization,' 'authority,' and others.

But in a narrower, more specific sense, there are two dilemmas that every manager faces that are solely concerned with directing one's own subordinates. The first arises from the beliefs that each person has about the nature of man, especially with regard to work. Do people like to work or must they be forced to work? Are people willing to take responsibility or do they shun it? This dichotomy of possibilities creates a dilemma for each manager. The methods the manager uses to direct subordinates are shaped by the answers to these questions.

The most famous statement of the above dichotomy was made by Douglas McGregor who entitled the two possibilities as Theory X and Theory Y.[12] He said that every manager holds one or the other of these two viewpoints as the manager's 'theory' of why subordinates act as they do. Furthermore, McGregor believed that most managers espoused Theory X.

Theory X states that: (1) people dislike to work inherently and will avoid work if they can; (2) therefore, people must be forced to work by the threat of punishment; (3) however, this is acceptable because people prefer to be directed as they have little ambition, wish to avoid responsibility, and seek security above all.

In contrast, Theory Y assumes that: (1) the effort of work is as natural to people as that of play; (2) internal controls of self-direction are as valid as external controls if people are committed to the objectives of the work; (3) commitment to objectives is a function of the associated rewards; (4) people can learn not only to accept responsibility, but to seek it; (5) the majority of people have the capacity to be imaginative, ingenuous, and creative; and (6) modern work conditions do not utilize much of the intellectual potential of people.

McGregor wanted every manager to adopt a Theory Y approach. By treating one's subordinates as mature, responsible people, he believed that benefits would accrue to the employee from improved morale and greater enthusiasm, to the manager from the opportunity to spend less time in close supervision, and to the organization from the increased creativity and productivity of both the employee and the manager.

However, McGregor also realized that most employees appeared to have the characteristics assigned to Theory X. Workers just do not seem to want to work. McGregor believed that this was an aberration that had become part of a 'vicious circle' that was now hard to break. It was an example of a self-justifying prophecy. That is, because managers in the past believed, for a variety of reasons, that workers were lazy and irresponsible, the workers were treated by the managers as if they were this in fact. In turn, because the workers were treated in this manner, they adopted the qualities expected of them — indolence and irresponsibility. After several generations of this, it had become a vicious circle, difficult to break.

But McGregor believed it could be broken if only managers would realize the error of their ways and try to break out of the circle — through adopting a Theory Y perspective. Other modern management theorists and consultants have agreed with McGregor and added their forces to promoting this outlook. They usually use a different name to describe it — management by objectives, democratic leadership, participative management — but they all amount to the same exhortation.

But can the practicing manager actually adopt Theory Y? And why should he or she do this? Will Theory Y necessarily improve productivity in all situations? Might it not lessen productivity in some situations, or even most situations? Does what is gained from a Theory Y perspective outweigh what is lost from turning away from Theory X? That is the dilemma in directing for each and every manager.

A 'Theory Y' approach, no matter what name it is called by, is a time-consuming approach for the manager. It calls for the manager to spend a great deal of time discussing the job with each individual employee, establishing individual targets and goals for a particular time-period for each employee, and monitoring each employee's performance at regular intervals to ensure that the trust and responsibility has been well-placed. It is individualized management. Therefore, it is also a much more subjective form of management as an appraisal must be made, and remade, of each employee's capabilities. It may well be a superior approach for the employee, although not every employee wants the associated responsibility, but it may not be a superior approach for the organization. That is, it assumes that what benefits the employee will necessarily benefit the organization. In fact, if one tried to compute costs and benefits, the figures for both can never be more than vague estimates.

On the other hand, the traditional, external controls of a Theory X-type approach are more objective, more equitable as all employees are treated the same, and therefore less discriminatory. However, as McGregor suggests, the approach is negative towards the employee and therefore disheartening to the manager. The employee tries only to avoid punishment, and the manager's time is occupied in ensuring that rules are obeyed.

The manager faces a dilemma between a perspective that is objective, uniform, non-discriminatory, and easier to implement, but possibly disheartening to both subordinates and superior, and a perspective that is subjective, individualized, inequitable, and more difficult to implement, but probably more motivating to everyone. Which perspective should the manager use for directing subordinates?

For example, the manager of a small department store in a country town believes mightily in Theory Y. He has four employees working for him, each supervising a particular section of the store — household goods, sporting goods, hardware, and stationery.

The lady in charge of household goods is very competent and well-organized; she knows what inventory she needs to hold and can judge immediately whether or not a new item from the suppliers will sell; she believes that 'merchandise sells itself.'

The man in charge of sporting goods is an ex-athlete; he is very adept at explaining the equipment so that the customer buys what he or she really needs, but has no head for figures and continually runs out of items.

The man in charge of hardware is an older man, a handyman who has built and repaired almost everything there is around a house; his department also runs out of items easily, but he is such a good innovator that he can find the customer a substitute that should work just as well.

The lady in charge of stationery is herself an ardent reader of books and writer of letters; she feels these are cultured pursuits that should be supported by quality merchandise, and stocks her shelves accordingly.

Each of the four supervisors has a different image of the store and its customers. Household goods sees it as a knick-knack store appealing to the masses; sporting goods, as a reputable establishment whose equipment fits the customer's needs; hardware, as a traditional do-it-yourself outlet of small purchases by weekend workers; stationery, as a quality store for ladies of substance. Each section of the store has built up a good following of customers who provide repeat business, but the town is large enough to have competitors for all four sections right there on the main street.

The manager has been told by the store's owner that the store's gross revenues are not sufficient. The owner wants a greater return. Both owner and manager are certain that the problem lies in the fact that there are really four stores in operation, not one. That is, each customer is attracted to only one section of the store, makes a limited purchase, and leaves. There is little or no intra-store traffic that would result in a customer buying several items from several different sections before leaving. Being Theory Y-oriented, the manager discusses the situation with each employee in turn.

The household goods supervisor says that she could stock more expensive, quality items that would attract the ladies from stationery, but she only has so much display space and the handy, everyday things would have to be restricted. This, in turn, could cause the 'masses' to go elsewhere and the store might have even less business than before.

The lady in stationery, on the other hand, does not believe that she should try to appeal to the 'masses' that buy the household goods. These people do not write letters, she says, and the trashy books they want to read would drive away her present clientele.

Both the ex-athlete and the hardware supervisor feel they could hold more inventory and so satisfy the present customers, but they wonder if the manager is prepared to undergo the additional expense. As for attracting customers from other sections, however, they see that as ridiculous. Women do not buy sporting goods nor hardware, and men make shopping trips for the one or the other, never both together. Given that situation, they see no prospect for improving the store's returns.

Unfortunately for the manager, the owner cares not a whit for Theory Y nor Theory X. All he wants are increased revenues and he does not accept the concerns of the four employees that the manager has relayed to him. The manager is in a quandary.

Each of his four employees accepts responsibility willingly, shows some creativity, is self-directed, and enjoys the work. But the overall result is disunity, a divergent image for the customers, and revenues that are less than maximum. Should the manager leave the situation as it is, acknowledging the responsibility and ability of the four employees? Or should he identify a store-wide norm derived from evaluating such factors as maximum revenue, minimum inventory cost, personalized selling, total appeal to customers, morale of supervisors, attractiveness of competitors, demands of owner, and the manager's own predilections about being a Theory Y person, and insist that the four employees meet that norm? Would it even be possible to derive a meaningful norm from such a wide variation of demands? A norm would be a compromise, but can there be a lasting compromise when there are such discrepancies in the objectives?

There is really no possibility for compromise in this dilemma. One either directs employees by a Theory Y approach and accepts the variety of consequences that will result, such as was illustrated by the department store. Or one directs employees with a Theory X perspective and gains uniformity at the cost of employee input and morale. Because individuals are not equal and do not perceive the same situation in an equivalent manner, treating them unequally can only result in an array of differences; on the other hand, treating them equally only forces them into an unnatural mold. It is a dilemma.

The second dilemma that arises for the manager from the directing of subordinates involves the moment at which the manager steps in and takes over if things are going wrong. In his explanation of Theory Y, McGregor insisted that each manager be informed at all times of the progress of the subordinate. This is why the Theory Y approach is individualized and time-consuming for the manager. McGregor was not suggesting that the manager sit back until the particular time-period was finished and then learn how well or how poorly the subordinate had performed. Theory Y management required the manager to keep abreast of developments throughout the time-period. If one waited for the end of the time-period to take corrective action, it might well be too late to rectify matters.

But which moment is the correct moment? That is the heart of the dilemma. If the manager intervenes too early, it indicates a lack of faith in the subordinate's abilities. No one gains confidence when a superior hovers around the work situation, glancing repeatedly over the worker's shoulder. If the manager moves in too soon, the individual may be destroyed. On the other hand, if the manager moves in too late, the organization may be destroyed. It does no good to lock the barn after the horse has been stolen.

For example, a supervisor of an accounting department decided to help one of the office secretaries move ahead in the organization by training her to be an administrative assistant. The important knowledge that she needed to obtain was an understanding of financial reporting: making journal entries, posting accounts, taking trial balances, working with a budget, and such like. It was a small firm and so while the regular accounting clerk was away on vacation, the secretary was to take full responsibility for the job. The supervisor spent a few hours explaining the work to her one Friday afternoon and she began on Monday morning. Since he had no difficulty understanding the work, he assumed that she would not either. She claimed that she was looking forward to Monday morning.

By Monday afternoon, she was a nervous wreck. She had interrupted him five times already that day to ask him how to handle different situations. He had stopped his work each time and carefully repeated the instructions to her, some of which were repetitious of Friday. Yet more situations were accumulating all the time and she lacked the confidence that she could handle them correctly. Surely she should not interrupt him again?

So she did not, and he, pleased that she was no longer asking him questions, left her alone for the next three weeks until the regular clerk returned.

The organization had not been destroyed by the time the regular clerk returned, but it was well on its way. Suppliers were already telephoning to inquire when their cheques were coming and other sections of the firm were demanding accurate statements of their budget. It took the regular clerk a week of nightly overtime to set things straight again, and the secretary returned to her letters mortified. She never again tried to be more than a secretary and soon transferred to a different company where her reputation was unknown.

The purpose of the example is not to fix blame. The only purpose is to ask the question — at what point should the supervisor have intervened? One would be justified in saying that the opportunity should never have been given in the first place, but one could also say that, since no harm was done in the long-term, it was simply a lesson well learned and the supervisor did right in not intervening at all.

Or, perhaps the supervisor should have realized from the five questions asked so quickly that the secretary did not have the confidence or ability for the work. In that case, he should have asked her if she needed help before that first Monday was over. Would she have said yes and admitted defeat? Or should he have waited until the end of the first Tuesday before asking her? What is the correct moment?

The dilemma exists because the situation requires two different sets of needs to be satisfied, the employee's and those of the organization. The desirable resolution would be to satisfy both sets simultaneously, a form of integration, but that is easier said than done. Compromise makes no sense in this dilemma while domination would mean probably that it would be the needs of the organization that should take precedence. That is, the manager should intervene too soon rather than too late. The ideal is to intervene at the correct time, neither too soon nor too late. To determine that moment, however, is not a simple calculation. It involves consideration of: 1) the employee's personality and psyche; 2) both the short-term and long-term needs of the organization for both profits and employee development; and 3) the manager's personality and psyche, too, including the manager's relationship with his or her own superior. McGregor never said that Theory Y management would be easy.

Notes

1. E.g., Don Hellriegel and John W. Slocum, Jr., *Management: A Contingency Approach* (Reading, MA: Addison-Wesley, 1974).
2. E.g., Harold Koontz and Cyril O'Donnell, *Management: A Systems and Contingency Analysis of Managerial Functions*.
3. E.g., Burt Scanlan and J. Bernard Keys, *Management and Organizational Behavior* (New York: John Wiley & Sons, 1979).
4. R. W. Morell, *Management: Ends and Means* (San Francisco, CA: Chandler, 1969), p. xii.

5. Herbert A. Simon, *The Shape of Automation for Men and Management*, p. 67.
6. The above example and the quotation were taken from: Daniel Madar, 'Foreign policy objectives, country studies and planning theory,' *Canadian Public Administration* XXIII (Fall, 1980), 380–99.
7. Cf. James A. F. Stoner, *Management* (Englewood Cliffs, N.J.: Prentice-Hall, 1978), pp. 131–33.
8. Luther Gulick, 'Notes on the Theory of Organization,' in *Papers on the Science of Administration*, ed. by Luther Gulick and L. Urwick (New York: Augustus M. Kelley, 1969), p. 15.
9. V. Seymour Wilson, 'The Relationship between Scientific Management and Personnel Policy in North American Administrative Systems,' *Public Administration* LI (Summer, 1973), 193–205.
10. Taken from T. J. Stevens, *The Business of Government* (Toronto: McGraw-Hill Ryerson, 1978), p. 134.
11. Charles E. Lindblom, 'The Science of "Muddling Through",' *Public Administration Review* XIX (Spring, 1959), 79–88.
12. Douglas McGregor, *The Human Side of Enterprise* (New York: McGraw-Hill, 1960), pp. 33–48.

CHAPTER 5

Dilemmas in the organization's external relationships

The previous chapters dealt with dilemmas that arise in the relationships that are internal to the organization. In those chapters, the organization was portrayed as if it were an autonomous, self-contained entity operating in isolation from the rest of society. Reality, of course, is not like this. Nor in fact would there be any continuous purpose for an organization were it not to interact with people and organizations external to itself.

This external area is often referred to as the organization's environment, but it is not the environment by itself that creates any dilemmas for the organization's decision-makers. The dilemmas are created by the relationships that these decision-makers establish with the community in which the organization functions. The goals that the decision-makers choose to pursue are not goals in isolation, but the result of choices between equally desirable outcomes, often in opposition to values held by some members of the community. Thus, they represent dilemmas.

Because these goals are in opposition to each other and because they are both desired within the community, on the one hand by organizational decision-makers, on the other hand by the general public, compromise will invariably be the chosen form of resolution. As was explained in Chapter One, integration is not feasible in situations like these. These are not dilemmas in means to *a* goal, but dilemmas amongst goals or ends.

Domination is not likely to be the form of resolution either. Both sides could try to dominate the other, but each recognizes that it needs the other, so that domination is somewhat suicidal. Organizational decision-makers require the general public as customers, employees, donors, shareholders, clients; the general public requires the organizational decision-makers to provide its required or desired goods and services. Symbiotic relationships do not flourish under domination.

Another reason that compromise has been sought invariably in the resolution of these dilemmas is that compromise has allowed the problems to disappear, usually quickly and easily. Imbued with the concept of the 'Golden Mean,' the citizens of Western nations are quick to attempt peaceable solutions through compromise. For example, the desire for clean air or clean water has led to the installation of anti-pollution devices by many different types of manufacturers. How well these devices work varies considerably from country to country and even within countries. But for most of the general public, the problem is now seen to be resolved and little further consideration is given to it. The general public became concerned when nothing was being done (i.e., domination by the manufacturers), but quickly left the problem to the managers of other regulatory organizations when some level of compromise was instituted. Because the majority of the general public live daily with compromises due to the choices thrust upon them for this item or that item, this purchase or that purchase, compromise is understood intuitively as a necessary and sufficient form of resolution. Compromises allow problems to disappear, at least for the time being.

This chapter is also the one chapter in the book where the clients or customers of the organization, the general public as they are often called, feel that they have a significant contribution to make. For the previous, 'internal' dilemmas, the general public is inclined usually to allow the organization to make its own decisions and regulate itself, as long as it acts within the law. The organization was portrayed as being autonomous.

In these 'external' dilemmas, however, the general public is much more likely to express a view as to how the organization should act. The initiative for this will come partly from social philosophers and other commentators and partly from the electorate and politicians who are aware that organizations influence their communities for better and for worse. The result is that these external dilemmas will often represent a conflict of purpose between the organization and the community. Top management then has a choice between: (1) aligning itself with the community; or (2) if it feels it is powerful enough, opposing the community; or (3) lobbying the politicians and the electorate in order to change the community's viewpoint. These alternatives do not in themselves represent a dilemma, but merely a choice of strategy.

Since Western industrial nations are riven with different ideologies and viewpoints as to how organizations should be controlled and who should do it, this could mean that this chapter would be the largest part of the book, elucidating literally dozens of vexing situations. Instead, less than half a dozen of these external dilemmas have been chosen. Their common factor is that these five dilemmas are in the hands of the top management or some other group within the organization for their resolution — and thus their place in this book. Western nations, in general, have statutes which establish guidelines for most of these areas of concern. It is then left to the individual organization to resolve the dilemma within the constraints of the guidelines. The constraints of the guidelines usually establish a minimum level which leaves considerable leeway for the organization, and thus the dilemma. There is lots of room for compromise.

For example, nations establish minimum wage laws and then leave each organization to determine how much more than the minimum each worker is to receive. The organization is faced with a dilemma. On the one hand, it could pay only the minimum wage and have a poorly motivated, unskilled workforce whose turnover will probably be high, but whose direct costs may be low. Alternatively, it could pay considerably more than the minimum wage and have a better motivated, more highly skilled workforce with lower turnover, but whose direct costs are much higher.

The example illustrates the nature of the dilemmas in this chapter. The organizational decision-makers have a set of dilemmas to resolve that are born of the expectations and the relationships between the members of the organization and the members of the larger community. The fact that an organizational decision-maker is at one and the same time a member of both the organization and the larger community only adds to the complexity. (However, that personal dilemma will not be explored in this book.)

Finally, the myriad of differing ideologies and viewpoints in Western industrialized nations will also make this chapter appear to be the shallowest in the book, as it is not the intent to deal with every possible facet of each of the five dilemmas, nor with all the relationships of these facets. The peoples of different nations will approach these five dilemmas with different goals and values, and therefore may not analyze them in exactly the same manner as they have been discussed here. There is little that can be done to overcome this except to write a complete treatise on each dilemma, and that is not the intent of this book. The author apologizes in advance to everyone who feels that the discussion has been biased unnecessarily or that sufficient weight has not been given to the merits of some argument. It is the intent in this chapter to deal with these five dilemmas in a general way such that they are made more real to decision-makers and students of organizations. As with all the dilemmas in this book, these latter people must then adapt the arguments to their own particular situations.

a. Social Responsibility

The concept of 'Social Responsibility,' of decision-makers in each organization acting in a manner that is responsive to the demands of the larger community and not just to the needs of the individual organization, is a concept that is ascribed commonly only to private sector organizations. The assumption is that public sector organizations are always socially responsible. However, the concept need not be limited to private sector organizations, supposedly torn between the dictates of the society and the dictates of the profit-and-loss statement. All organizations face this dilemma, be they businesses, government departments, charities, universities, unions, or whatever.

The social responsibility dilemma pits the direct claimants for the benefits of the organization against the indirect claimants. Since every organization is a part of a larger community, all have both types of claimants. (The obverse of this dilemma, the amount of participation by these claimants in the operations of the organization, will be examined in the next section of this chapter.)

Direct claimants are those people who receive immediate benefits from the operations of the organization. These people may be customers, employees, or shareholders of a corporation; they may be either employees or farmers if the organization is a government department of agriculture; they may be donors, employees, or recipients if the organization is a charity. It is difficult to define and delimit a direct claimant because benefits are not always financial nor even tangible. The common factor is that a direct claimant will be known to the organization by name; there will be a record of that person somewhere in the organization.

Indirect claimants are everyone else in the community, or the nation, or even, as some social philosophers will claim, in the world. They create the dilemma for the organization. Organizations are assumed to have a responsibility toward their direct claimants. How much responsibility must they exhibit towards their indirect claimants?

The traditional viewpoint, arising out of nineteenth century, laissez-faire liberalism, is that the organization not only has no responsibility toward the indirect claimants, it should not have any either. This viewpoint makes the case that the only purpose of an organization is to maximize the benefits to its direct claimants.[1] Were a business to spend its money on a socially responsible action such as sponsoring a symphony concert, for example, this action would decrease the benefits it could provide to the direct claimants. In effect, the business would be taxing these direct claimants. Customers would be paying the equivalent of a sales tax since otherwise the business could lower its price for the item; or employees would be paying the equivalent of an income tax since otherwise they could receive higher wages; or shareholders would be paying the equivalent of a capital tax since otherwise they could receive larger dividends.

The traditional viewpoint is associated usually with the actions of businesses and then claims that a business has no right to be levying taxes. However, to the extent that a non-profit organization spends part of its funds to subsidize community activities, it, too, could be said to be levying a tax on its direct claimants. As examples, a children's charity might provide funds to help a circus come to town; a union might give money to a community library. In both these examples, more money has to be provided to these non-profit organizations in order to provide the same level of benefits to the direct claimants. This could be said to be the equivalent of a tax upon these direct claimants, or upon the donors as the case might be.

In short, the traditional viewpoint states that the decision-makers of every organization should limit their responsibility to the direct claimants of the organization. The leaders of each organization owe their responsibility strictly to that organization and not to the larger community. These leaders are not hired to improve directly the community; they are hired to care for the direct interests of the particular organization. There are other organizations whose function is to improve directly the community; social responsibility should be left to the leaders of these other organizations and they, in turn, can tax

accordingly the whole community, if necessary. The traditional viewpoint demands that 'each shoemaker should stick to his last.'

The opposing viewpoint says that that traditional viewpoint is outmoded and antiquated. Its proponents believe that organizations in the twentieth century cannot and should not be managed in the manner that nineteenth century organizations were. It says that the modern organization is a functioning part of its community and must adopt a socially responsible attitude toward that community.[2] This viewpoint claims that, in order to have a decent community, it is necessary for all members to make contributions to community welfare without any expectation of a direct benefit in return. For example, a business may well have to sponsor a symphony concert if there is no other source of funds within the community. Furthermore, to the extent that the customers, employees, and shareholders of the business attend the concert, they are direct beneficiaries of this socially responsible action by the business.

Opponents of this modern viewpoint would counter this last argument by saying that the money should have gone to one or all of these three direct claimants in the first place, instead of being kept from them without their say in the matter. These people then could spend the money as they saw fit, perhaps on the concert, perhaps not.

However, the modern viewpoint would note that there probably would have been no concert without the sponsorship of the business. Because of their size, corporations can do things quickly and easily with large grants of money that would require a lot of long and arduous work if it were to be done by individuals. Very few private citizens have the money or the time to sponsor a full symphony concert. Furthermore, the publicity that the business gained from sponsoring the concert may well lead to improved sales for the business which, in turn, could have direct benefits for the employees and shareholders, and even the customers through lower prices in the future. Sponsorship can be considered to be just a cost of doing business, like advertising.

However, it is very difficult, if not impossible, to determine accurately the benefits of advertising. This fact leads to the crux of the dilemma. How can the results of socially responsible actions be computed accurately? The traditional viewpoint says that they cannot and therefore the only honest approach is to avoid trying.

The modern viewpoint says that the benefits must be taken on faith and therefore the actions must be undertaken even without an accurate accounting. More importantly, this viewpoint says that good citizenship means that everyone should participate in promoting community welfare: business executives, union leaders, directors of charities, as well as the politicians, newspaper editors, school teachers, or social philosophers that have been entrusted traditionally with this. In fact, this viewpoint would contend that business executives have every bit as much right and knowledge to contribute to the community as do these traditional participants. What gives these traditional participants the expertise to decide the community's values? If business executives do not express their opinions, who will speak for them?

The traditional viewpoint says merely that no one has to — business executives should simply direct their businesses and be social commentators on their private time.

For the decision-maker in the organization, the resolution of this dilemma will probably be a compromise. Modern communities demand socially responsible actions by executives and most organizational executives agree with this philosophy. The question is — how much? No organization is expected to be so socially responsible that it gives away all its resources and ceases to exist. None is even expected to jeopardize its existence through these actions. That extreme is beyond anyone's intentions.

On the other hand, citizens do not look kindly on an organization that is perceived to have no social conscience, that merely meets the minimum standard and answers only to its direct claimants. Citizens know that even the indirect claimants are affected by the operations of the organization and that there must be some recompense by the organization. For example, even a person who cannot drive a car is affected by the actions and operations of the automobile manufacturers, the oil companies, the departments of highways, and other organizations. The citizen, the indirect claimant, may give these organizations their due, but not to the total disregard and neglect of the citizen's concerns. The organizational leader must compromise to some extent.

The closest that any Western nation has come to establishing a minimum standard for social responsibility is to credit organizations with income tax deductions for their charitable works. However, this is not really a minimum as it does not force all organizations to be socially responsible; it only rewards those that are.

For those organizations that do not pay income taxes, nations require that their expenditures should be limited to the activities for which they were created. Unions should work solely for their members; charities for their clientele; government departments for the particular citizens who qualify for their programs. However, that merely resurrects the dilemma. How is it to be decided as to which activities are acceptable and which are not, and which people are direct claimants and which are not? As a government tourism department, for example, attempts to tell all potential tourists about its services, it surely has to spend money on people that have no intention of being tourists. Similarly, the union that builds a community library will benefit non-union citizens, even if it bars these people from the reading room; the union members who do use the library will become more knowledgeable citizens, and probably more productive.

Extreme answers represent domination and are unworkable in this dilemma. There must be both a measure of social responsibility and a measure of responsibility to the organization. Integration, since one viewpoint denies the merits of the other, is also impossible. Social responsibility can only be obtained at the expense of responsibility to the direct claimants, and vice versa. Compromise is left, but the amount of compromise cannot be predetermined. The result is that the dilemma will occur over and over again and must be resolved anew each time a situation arises.

b. Participation

It is one thing for an organization to provide benefits to its direct claimants, and even its indirect ones, it is quite another thing to determine who should decide what those benefits will be, and the recipients of them. Are the top-level decision-makers the ones to decide, or the employees as well, or the shareholders, or the citizenry at large? (There is some similarity between this dilemma and that of 'the locus of decision-making' in Chapter Two; here, however, the concern is with groups external to the organizational hierarchy, not the middle- and lower-level managers within it.) Every organization faces the dilemma of 'participation,' of determining whose opinions carry the most weight in making the decisions that give the organization its purpose.

In a corporation, the dilemma usually pits the shareholders against top-level management, but 'industrial democracy' or 'worker participation' could place the employees against top-level managers. In a union, it is the members against the union leaders. In the government, it is the politicians versus the citizenry, and, within the government departments, the top-level civil servants versus the citizens, or pressure groups, or lower-level employees, or even the politicians. In churches, it is the lay members against the ministry. There is no organization that does not face the dilemma of who shall participate in decision-making, and how and when.

One could suggest that if all the above opposing groups worked together in cooperation, there would be no problems. If the 'versus' was replaced by 'with' in each situation, would there be a dilemma? The answer is that there still would be. There is no question that the working conditions might be more peaceful if the 'versus' was removed. However, the dilemma would remain. Two sides are created in each situation because of differing interests, differing expertise, and differing responsibilities. For example, the church minister is a full-time, paid employee who has spent years studying theology and church doctrine and who has been hired legally to do a job. The members of the congregation cannot match these characteristics, no matter how much both sides would wish that there be cooperation and smooth, peaceful operations. The question remains of how much participation should there be by members of the congregation.

This is a dilemma of democracy versus expediency. Proponents of democracy contend that every person who is affected by the results of a decision should have the opportunity to participate in the making of that decision. This would be as valid for the political system of a nation as for the operations of a business or the purchase of books for a community library. Furthermore, many would contend that having a vote on these issues is not a sufficient opportunity for participation. True democracy would require that each person has an adequate length of time to voice opinions, ask questions, and attempt to convince others of his or her beliefs and viewpoint. (A sub-problem of the democratic perspective is to determine how the decision is to be adopted — by majority vote, unanimity, or some other measurement — but that issue is not necessarily pertinent to this dilemma.)

Those who oppose participative democracy do so usually on the basis of expediency. That is, they would contend that the type of democracy that is being demanded is slow, wasteful, and amateurish. It is slow in that it extends the length of time before a decision can be made; it is wasteful in that it requires money to be spent for explanation and discussion which may not make any difference to the eventual decision; it is amateurish in that the vote of a person who knows little about the issue is equal to the vote of an expert who specializes in studying that issue. For example, most citizens are exasperated when the agreements reached by union leaders in their negotiations with management must then be ratified by the total union membership before the agreements can be implemented. Are not the union leaders experts enough that they can speak for their members? Is the ideal of democracy really worth the extra time, trouble, and cost of the ratification which is so often 'a rubber-stamp'?

But a ratification is not always 'a rubber-stamp.' How can a community predetermine which decisions need a democratic resolution and which can be left to organizational leaders to make on its behalf? It cannot, of course, so what happens is that most citizens leave those decisions to the organizational leaders for those matters with which they agree or are unconcerned, and demand participation when the decision affects them personally and adversely. However, that is scarcely a principled rationale. Whether or not one's ox is being gored cannot be a guiding principle for a community because, as was noted with the dilemma of social responsibility, the distinction between direct and indirect claimant is often arbitrary.

For example, one person may feel that the elimination of a bus route is a good thing, but does not affect that person and so can be left to the community leaders to decide. However, a neighbour, who is equally unaffected in the present, believes that the elimination may have dire consequences for the neighbourhood sometime in the future. How much say should this second person have at this present moment in time? Is this second person a direct claimaint? Furthermore, if this neighbour is allowed any say at the present, does that delay not infringe upon the rights of the first person who wants the bus route eliminated now? When is participation an ideal and when is it a delaying tactic? Is it democratic participation that the community is achieving, or merely manipulation by an organized and vocal minority?

As was noted in Chapter Two, participation within an organization is no less a dilemma. In the interests of expediency and legality, organizational leaders normally are accorded the authority to make decisions for the organization. However, every organizational leader will recognize that decisions that are not made with the support of the people who will implement them are difficult if not impossible to enact. The expertise of technocracy must be blended with the enthusiasm of democracy. This includes people outside the organization, too, and one problem associated with this dilemma is to determine who should be considered a member of the organization.

For example, the literature on organizations differentiates between people-processing organizations and people-changing organizations. An immigration department that issues passports, a business that makes paring knives by the thousands, a charity that issues receipts for every donation can all be considered to be people-processing organizations. There may well be no face-to-face contact between these organizations and their clients.

But there are also organizations that attempt to change their customers or clients, change their attitudes and behaviour such that the clients will act differently in the future. Some obvious examples are schools, churches, universities, manpower training departments, welfare services, libraries, and such businesses as doctors, dentists, lawyers, radio stations, newspapers, and, of course, marketing agencies. There are also many organizations whose operations lie in a gray area between the two extremes, both processing and changing people. Automobile manufacturers are one example, as are most organizations involved with transportation and communication, to name only a couple of industrial examples.

What should be the perspective towards the clients and customers of these organizations? Are these people outside the organization? Or are they on the bottom level of the organizational chart, subordinate to the workers in the total hierarchy? Or should they even be placed at the top of the hierarchy with the rest of the organization subservient to them? Is it important to give these people access to the decisions made within the organization (democracy) or is it sufficient to merely provide a service to them (expediency and expertise)? Are these clients and customers a part of the organization or are they external to it? Are they participants or recipients? The answers to these questions, which the decision-makers of each organization must give, will determine to a great extent the approach they have to resolving the dilemma of participation.

Once again, however, the question is not one of 'either-or,' but 'how much?' How much democracy before expediency is foregone? How much participation can be tolerated before effective expertise is destroyed?

To resolve this dilemma, integration is again meaningless; one goal denies the merits of the other. There cannot be both total participation and total expertise on the parts of both insiders and outsiders. Each side has to have some measure of expertise and some measure of participation, but it is impossible for it to have all. Usually, the people within the organization will have the greater expertise; the people outside the organization may well have the greater concern about the results.

So, too, is domination unworkable. The extreme of total participation by outsiders makes a mockery of the responsibilities of organizational leaders, and the extreme of no participation from outside is abhorrent to the organizational claimants. Compromise remains.

Each organization must compromise and resolve this dilemma over and over again as new concerns arise. The adoption of generalized policies which can be formulated in advance is an attempt to eliminate the reoccurrence of this dilemma. However, the generalized procedures cannot possibly foresee the variety of issues that will arise, nor the intensity of concern for each one. For example, the annual killing of seal pups off the coast of Newfoundland is protested vigorously some years, and not at all in others. Even generalized procedures will be questioned in specific situations when not everyone will agree that the general procedure is or is not applicable to the dispute that has arisen.

To force some measure of compromise, Western industrialized nations have attempted to establish minimum standards for particular organizations to cover this dilemma. For example, business corporations are required to hold annual meetings of shareholders; unions are required to have contracts ratified; governments are required to hold referendums for certain matters; non-profit societies must also have annual meetings. Above and beyond these minimums, however, the nations are silent. It is left to the senior executives of each organization to decide for themselves how much more participation is desirable and possible before their role as decision-makers is negated. Participation is a constant dilemma.

c. Professionalism

As industrialization increases in each nation, two related forces operate to create another dilemma for top-level managers. The first force is the ever-increasing specialization within occupations; the second force is the increasing size of organizations, such that it becomes more and more practical for organizations to employ these specialists rather than to contract for their services with an outside firm. For each one of these hired specialists that is a professional — such as a doctor, a lawyer, an engineer, an accountant, an actuary, a social worker — the organization introduces a dilemma into its midst, almost like a Trojan Horse.

This is because a true professional will not have just the interests of the organization at heart. Any professional must give allegiance to four interests: (1) to the customer or client; (2) to the community represented by the certifying government; (3) to the profession; and (4) to oneself and one's family. The organizational professional must add a fifth allegiance, an allegiance to the organization as well. Which of the five allegiances is to take precedence in any situation? How are the top-level managers to use the professional to the best advantage of the organization?

For example, if a life assurance company is large enough, it may employ a company doctor to ascertain the health of applicants who wish to have policies on their lives. This doctor examines a particular applicant and concludes that the person is unlikely to live very long. If the doctor has the best interests of the client at heart, the doctor should recommend that the client obtain as much life insurance as possible. On the other hand, to the life assurance company, the doctor should recommend that it not issue a policy on the applicant's life. The premium could not possibly cover the pay-out.

But as well, if the doctor has any allegiance to the medical profession, he or she will realize that one opinion on the matter is not sufficient and therefore recommend that the applicant be examined by another doctor at least. However, this third potential recommendation, if implemented, would cost the community extra money through the health service, and so may be contrary to the doctor's allegiance to the community. Which recommendation should the doctor make? Should the primary allegiance be to the company, the client, the community, or the profession? Can the top-level managers predetermine which allegiance should have priority since they, too, have allegiance not only to the life assurance company, but also to its clients, and to the general community?

Another example concerns a professional engineer who inspects the building of roads and bridges for a government Department of Highways. At the completion of one bridge, he determines that the bridge, while safe enough now, has not been built according to specifications and therefore might develop problems sometime in the future. He notes this in his report, but before the report is made public, he is asked to delete those comments. He is told by his chief that those comments will reflect unfavourably on both the engineers who built the bridge and the political authorities who authorized its construction. Besides, the bridge is now safe and the engineer has no proof that anything untoward will actually happen in the future.

The engineer feels that if he does not note the discrepancies in his report, he has no right to be considered a professional engineer anymore. However, when he discusses the situation with his wife, she reminds him that, should he decide to quit over the matter, unemployment in the area is high and his two teenaged children are at the stage when they are incurring large expenses. Where should the engineer's allegiance lie? What should he decide to do?

Furthermore, what should the senior people in the Department of Highways do? Should they be insisting that the duty of the department to the political authorities take precedence? Or should they be protective of the group of employees who built the bridge? Or should they be supportive of the professional engineer who inspected the bridge? Or is their prime concern the citizens of the community who will use the bridge? And if it is, will this concern be better demonstrated by releasing knowledge of the discrepancies, or by hiding it? Finally, what is the duty of the senior people of the Department of Highways to the engineering profession, itself, from which they obtain so large a proportion of their technical employees? Should they be upholding its standards, even when their own employees have fallen short of them?

A similar situation arises in those organizations where employees are unionized. Union members do not have as many potential allegiances as do professionals, but they still face a potential conflict amongst duty to the union, duty to the organization and their employer, and duty to themselves and their families. And indeed, as more and more occupations become highly specialized and seek out the accoutrements of professions, top-level managers can only find this dilemma increasing in importance for the organization. Lucky is he who has only two masters.

For the organization, the resolution of the dilemma will depend largely on the personality of the professional involved. The company doctor will make a recommendation according to his or her values and judgement about the particular situation. The professional engineer will do likewise. What the top-level manager should be doing is attempting to create an attitude of trust and support within the organization such that the professional can make the recommendation without feeling threatened.

To do otherwise is not a proper resolution. There is a great temptation to use domination to resolve this dilemma, for all senior decision-makers to demand that allegiance to the organization take precedence over all else. The threat is made that if the professional does not give priority to the organization, then the professional should quit and work elsewhere. It is a hollow threat. It accomplishes little. It takes a complex situation of utmost significance to the professional who is wrestling with it, and resolves it simplistically like cutting through a Gordian Knot.

Senior managers who insist on the priority of the demands of the organization in all situations will have inferior professionals working for them. If that is what they want, so be it, but their insistence on domination belies their capacities as responsible decision-makers. They will have company doctors who neglect to maintain their medical knowledge and skills, engineers who will 'cut corners' without concern for safety, accountants who are unconcerned about the development of new approaches, social workers whose bureaucratic severity will intimidate the clients who need their help. But the community will decide that the acceptable minimum must be at a higher level than that, and the senior managers will have to respond. Therefore, domination of the organizational interest is not sufficient.

Nor is integration a valid possiblity. If the professional can align the decision with all the allegiances, that is good, but it shows only that there is no problem, no dilemma, present. The problems arise because the allegiances cannot be all satisfied simultaneously. Integration is not a possibility in these situations. Someone or some body is going to have to accept second-best.

A compromise will have to be reached within the organization. An atmosphere must be created within the organization such that the various allegiances of the professional are respected, including the organizational allegiance. Sometimes the professional will have to make concessions, especially if peer professionals disagree with his or her proposal; sometimes it will have to be the senior managers who concede, who alter the demands of the organization, even at an additional cost. This cannot be helped if a spirit of compromise is to be maintained. However, the active professional will recognize the atmosphere of trust that pervades the organization. Problem situations that arise will be no less complex, but they will be resolved in a spirit of cooperation that recognizes all the allegiances that are present. In the long-run, the organization cannot lose. Professionalism is a growing phenomenon, not a diminishing one, and organizational decision-makers must learn to compromise with it.

d. Efficiency

Throughout the 1970s, there was a renewed interest in an old bugaboo of organizational management, that of organizational efficiency. The concept of efficiency was contrasted usually with that of effectiveness. Managers were then encouraged to be both efficient and effective. Peter Drucker is considered to have made the most succinct definition of these two concepts: efficiency means doing things right, while effectiveness means doing the right thing.[3] Drucker claimed that effectiveness was the more important of the two. Efficiency was important, but should only be sought after the organization had determined first what it was it should be doing.

A more intricate definition was formulated by Al Johnson, who equated efficiency with administrative efficiency; effectiveness, with policy efficiency; and introduced a third aspect, service efficiency.[4] Administrative efficiency was what people usually meant when they discussed efficiency. It dealt with the production process that maximized the outputs for the given inputs. However, like Drucker, Johnson believed that administrative efficiency was of little significance if policy efficiency (such matters as proper plant location, best production process, sufficient market for output) had not been resolved first. But even if it had, service efficiency, or the constraints imposed by democratic governments, could negate either of those first two types of efficiency and therefore had overwhelming precedence.

For example, an analysis of administrative efficiency might discover that the mail cannot be delivered throughout a country at a price low enough to be acceptable to the citizens and high enough to cover the costs. However, the politicians, looking at policy efficiency, might decide that mail service is a necessary requirement of modern countries and therefore has to be delivered, no matter the cost to the nation. This said, service efficiency comes into consideration because that mail must then be delivered equitably throughout the nation, not just to people who will pay a high price or who live in cities where administrative efficiency can flourish and keep the costs as low as possible. That is, administrative efficiency, the type of efficiency that is thought of normally, is only important if the right policies have been chosen first and the constraints of service efficiency have been acknowledged.

The example is not restricted to the public sector. Businesses and other private organizations also face the constraints of service efficiency. Anti-pollution devices must be fitted onto exhaust vents; hiring practices cannot be discriminatory; products must be labelled adequately and cannot contain banned substances. The private sectors of Western industrialized countries face an ever-increasing number of regulations imposed on the production of goods and services, and so must consider service efficiency, too. The dilemma arises from the desire to achieve administrative and policy efficiencies while being subjected to a contrary demand, service efficiency. (As will be explained later in this section, that the private sector can often pass on to the customer the extra costs created by the service efficiency regulations is not relevant to the resolution of this dilemma.)

Another way of looking at this dilemma is in terms of quantity versus quality. Both administrative efficiency and policy efficiency are quantity-oriented concepts. They seek to maximize the outputs in comparison to a given set of inputs. Alternatively, they seek to lower the costs of the inputs necessary to make a given set of outputs. Either approach has to lead to a lessening of the quality of the good or service. More output for a given input has to lower the quality of each item; lower costs for the inputs have to make each item more inferior (assuming in both cases that the production process was efficient in both policy and administrative terms prior to the new demands). To what extent should consumers have to forego long-term quality of an item for the short-term gains of inferior, but cheaper, items? That is the dilemma.

Administrative and policy efficiency may well be only short-term advantages to a nation. It may seem that the nation is further ahead by having cheaper items for consumers to buy, such as mass-produced automobiles. However, if the cars have to be scrapped every two years and the nation has only a limited amount of metal, glass, and rubber, then in the long-term this emphasis on quantity is actually inefficient. Similarly, medical examinations could be more administratively efficient by reducing the time allowed to one minute. Many more people could then be examined by even fewer doctors, but what would be the quality of the examination?

On the other hand, an over-emphasis on quality may lead to a set of goods and services that only rich people could afford. Each automobile would be crafted so carefully that there would be very few ever produced.Or, each doctor would spend so long with each patient that many patients might die before they ever moved up the queue for their chance. Somehow, a balance must be drawn between quality and quantity, between service efficiency and the other two types, between the demands of the community for long-term responsibility in resource use and the demands of the organizations for short-term financial considerations, profits or budgets.

For Drucker, there is no compromise required between effectiveness and efficiency. One should determine the right thing to do (effectiveness), and then do it right (efficiency). However, it is the Johnson perspective that is preferred here. That is, even if the right thing to do has been determined, there are constraints on how efficiently one can do it. These constraints may be imposed either by the community or by the internal dynamics of the organization — such factors as its personnel, technology, financial resources, location. The constraints imposed by the community are the consideration in this section. They create an external, environmental dilemma for the organization.

Once again, Western industrialized nations have sought a compromise solution in resolving this dilemma. The private sectors are permitted to pursue the goals of quantity and efficiency if they so wish, but the nations use their regulatory mechanisms to ensure that a minimum standard of quality is built into the product or service. Examples abound — anti-pollution devices, standards of food and drink, building codes, professional practices.

Domination — the insistence of quality over quantity (or vice versa) — is not an appropriate solution in Western nations. Much good has resulted for consumers from allowing mass production methods to increase quantity at the expense of some quality. Like the first three dilemmas in this chapter, the problem is in determining at what point to stop — the minimum acceptable standard of 'some quality.' How much? It is better that all citizens can keep warm with a cheaply-made woolen blanket rather than having some citizens snug inside heavy wool blankets while the majority are naked.

But nor is the domination of quantity at the expense of quality an acceptable resolution. As nations realize that more and more natural resources are finite, not infinite, a short-term perspective on quantity and efficiency may be seen to be inefficient in the long-term. For example, the slash-and-burn agricultural methods of many developing nations are efficient in the short-run for clearing and fertilizing land, but wasteful and inefficient in the long-run when no trees are left and the soil has been eroded away.

Resolution of the dilemma through integration would seek to have both maximum quality and maximum quantity in our goods and services. It would be the superior resolution but it is logically impossible for all items or even any one item. As was argued before in this section, quantity and efficiency can only be obtained and maximized at the expense of quality. Resolution by compromise remains.

Instead of integration, what happens is that Western nations produce a variety of combinations of quality and quantity for any one item. For example, there are cheaply-made woolen blankets, produced efficiently but with little quality; there are better-made woolen blankets; and there are high-quality blankets of cashmere or other materials in very limited quantities. Consumers choose the blanket they can afford. A compromise is achieved.

The costs of the regulations or service efficiency imposed by the nation have some relevance to the dilemma, but are not normally of paramount consideration to its resolution. To the greatest extent possible, producers build these costs into the price of the good or service so that they are merely a constant added to all items. If a competitor from outside the nation does not bear these extra costs and therefore eliminates the domestic producer, then the costs are obviously of paramount consideration. In these cases, if there is no relief by the nation, then domination has occurred, not compromise, as the nation has allowed service efficiency or quality to eliminate quantity. But the more likely situation is for a compromise as the nation reduces some of its service efficiency requirements in order to allow the domestic producers to compete with foreigners. For example, American automobile manufacturers were allowed to reduce the quality of their pollution emission controls in order to lower the price of the cars and so allow these cars to be competitive with foreign-made ones.

The practice of a variety of combinations is a compromise resolution. The nation obtains both some quality and some quantity though this practice, and the individual consumer receives a compromise of the two depending upon which type of item was bought. New outputs, new products or services, can be obtained from a different set of inputs. However, for any given set of inputs, either quantity or quality must be sacrificed to improve the other. Quantity and efficiency are one goal; quality and service are another.

e. Change

Within every organization, there are two opposing forces at work. One force works towards growth, change, and innovation; the other, towards stability, continuity, and repetition. Both forces are necessary and desirable. It is no resolution to the resulting dilemma to attempt to abolish the one force or the other.

In systems parlance, the forces are referred to as the need for an adaptive mechanism and for a maintenance mechanism. The latter is considered by many writers to be a conservative force, reactionary and unbending, and therefore to be despised. However, this attitude sells it short.

The maintenance mechanism is the force that pursues administrative efficiency, that seeks to do things with as little effort as possible. It makes use of the lessons that have been learned from experience, and endeavours to repeat that experience with few changes. Assembly line workers produce the same types of products over and over again with the same motions; lecturers repeat their classes year after year with approximately the same set of notes; ministers conduct the church service each Sunday in the same manner and often with the same prayers and sermons; public servants process similar applications using the same rules and procedures. The maintenance mechanism keeps the organization from reinventing the wheel and allows costs to be minimized through repetition of performance. If one needs to go each day from A to B, one chooses the most efficient route and normally repeats it ever afterwards.

This is not to say, however, that people are by nature conservative, unchanging seekers of monotonous duplication. How was it decided to go to B in the first place and not to C or D? And how were all the alternative routes discovered that allowed the most efficient to be chosen? It is said to take three years of preparation, of adaptation and innovation, before the first automobile rolls off an assembly line; it takes months and even years of research and preparation before the lecturer can present the first class, and this is just as true for the religious minister; for the public servant, the adaptive mechanism has been at work, determining what new bills must be put through the legislative process, long before the maintenance mechanism comes into its own. One should not fault all these people for converting their efforts to maintenance after they have exerted so much in the adaptive stage.

Every organization must have both an adaptive mechanism and a maintenance one. Without the former, the organization is soon left behind by its competitors, making the cheapest buggy-whips when all the customers are driving cars. But without a maintenance mechanism, the organization is also left behind by its competitors, incurring high costs as it tackles each situation as if it were new and unique. The order of hymns, prayers, and sermon within a church service that was not repeated each week would drive most of the congregation elsewhere in their quest for stability and tranquility. Lecturers who never repeated themselves would have no time for research and would soon be out-of-date in their fields. Department store managers who perennially relocated the merchandise or who purchased from different suppliers each time or who altered the credit procedures each month would quickly lose both their customers and their employees. It is foolish advice to suggest that modern organizations must be adaptive and innovative as if that were the only requirement.

For the organization, and for the community, the complexity in this dilemma of balancing the two forces derives from the fact that organizations habitually assign these two mechanisms to different personnel. The maintenance mechanism is assigned normally to lower-level employees; the adaptive mechanism, to their managers or even to staff advisors. (There are many similarities between this dilemma and ones discussed previously in Chapters Three and Four.)

With this assignment, the principle of 'management by exception' comes into use. All situations that can be routinized are assigned to the subordinates, with the authority to undertake whatever action the situation requires. Those situations that are unique are then passed from the subordinate to the manager when they arise. The manager only handles the exceptions.

In most organizations, this would appear to leave each manager with a great deal of free time. The exceptional circumstances do not arise very often or else they would not be exceptional. How should the manager use this free time? The manager cannot be seen to be sitting around twiddling thumbs, and the industrious manager would not want to anyway. By the demands of our Western industrialized, liberal nations, the managers should be using this time to be creative, innovative, adaptive. Change is demanded continually by the shareholders, by the customers, and by the actions of competitors. The change dilemma is built into the system.

If the manager is not seeking change, planning alterations to the products, to the production processes, to the delivery system, or contemplating new products, new programs, new uses for the resources, then the nation questions his or her right to hold that position. However, if the manager does seek constantly to innovate and change, then extra pressures are applied continually to the lower-level employees upholding the maintenance mechanism. The dilemma creates a continuing tension for the organization. It also creates it for the community which both expects the old that the citizens have come to rely on, and the new which signals progress.

For example, a prominent fund-raising organization began at the 'grass roots' level with local committees of volunteers conducting different types of short-term campaigns. In order to achieve the most publicity throughout the country and in order to allow each local committee to benefit from the knowledge gained by the other local committees, a national organization was created after a few years. As a permanent secretariat, the national body operated on a year-round basis, so its staff were hired and were not volunteers. These staff people soon came to coordinate all the local campaigns so that they occurred across the country at the same time. In turn, this produced better publicity as the campaigns became national events.

Within a few years, the fund-raising campaigns were routinized to occur at three times during the year. The national staff sent out the required supplies at the appropriate times and the volunteers operated as the maintenance mechanism. Within the national office, a few staff looked after the shipment of supplies and the receipt of the funds, while the other staff, the managers, were there to look after any problems. Of course, the salaries for these managers came from the funds raised throughout the country. Both donors and volunteers soon began to ask what the managers were doing. Were more funds being raised each year? How did the managers justify their salaries? Planning, preparation, and evaluation of these three campaigns did not take that much time.

So the national managers undertook to plan other events throughout the year, an adaptive element to complement the maintenance element of the three campaigns. These new events were often unique or one-time campaigns, a cross-country tour by a singing group, for example, or a new wrinkle added to one of the three campaigns to see if more money could be raised. However, these events and additions always relied on volunteers in the local committees for implementation.

Many of these volunteers did not appreciate the changes and innovations. For these volunteers, it had been difficult enough to undertake each of the three annual campaigns and still meet commitments to families, friends, and jobs. Now the volunteers were being asked to undertake other campaigns, so that they, too, were being drawn into an almost year-round commitment. For many, the strain was too much and they quit helping the organization at any time. Others made the decision to restrict their assistance to one campaign each year. Some local committees tried to cope by hiring local people on a year-round basis, too, but other volunteers resented this and quit in protest. If new volunteers could have been found to undertake these adaptations, there would have been much less of a problem, but this happened only rarely.

The charity has continued to raise more funds each year. Indeed, the community demands this from its fund-raising organizations, as do the volunteers and other members. Without the national managers, this is unlikely to have occurred. However, there is also much resentment of the national managers by many of the local volunteers who believe that the managers do not appreciate the problems of the volunteers in the field. The organization spends a great deal of effort every year trying to recruit new volunteers. Some of the national staff, in turn, resent what they consider to be apathy on the part of local volunteers and so they plan new events which will raise funds without relying on volunteers. The charity struggles on, attempting to overcome the dilemma without realizing it is inherent to any organization.

The strains in the above example are not caused simply by the fact that the subordinates are volunteers. The same types of strains are exhibited in all organizations where one set of employees has specific duties to perform while another set of employees is charged with finding new duties. Some examples are: bank tellers whose routines are disrupted by new promotions in order to compete with other banks; airline clerks who must constantly learn new fares for different classes of passengers; government clerks who must adapt their operations to new tax rates. All are examples of the change dilemma inherent to every job, every organization, every life. Every employee can tolerate some innovation and adaptation into his or her work routine. The problem is in determining how much can be tolerated before the breaking point is reached. Unfortunately, this quantity will vary from person to person as it includes reference to the individual's genetic make-up, the job environment, and the non-work situation that each lives. Each manager will have to determine the quantity of change that can be handled by each subordinate.

Nor is this dilemma solely an internal one for the organization. Customers come to expect and rely on certain products and services being available for ever and ever, such as a special hair shampoo, a type of bread, an automobile model, a school for children, or even a government welfare program. They resent the organization which suddenly changes their lives by doing away with any of these. On the other hand, they also resent the failure of organizations to introduce new products and services, especially if they know these changes exist in other countries or other cities. People want not only the type of bread they have come to depend on, but also innovative types for special occasions or those times when one feels the need for a change. The organization is expected to provide both at all times. The dilemma comes from trying to satisfy the two opposing needs. The old loaf cannot be made nor eaten at the same time as the new one.

But this dilemma is not just a problem for customers and subordinates. Managers, too, desire a certain amount of routine which too much innovation or change can upset. For example, a young appliance repairman in a city of 200,000 people decided to stop working for the major appliance repair firm and establish his own firm. His personalized service and the speed with which he responded to calls soon gave him a good reputation and all the business he and his assistant could handle. As the word spread about the quality of his work, his reputation grew. As time passed, more and more people telephoned directly to him and ignored the major appliance repair firm. Eventually, he found himself with more business than he could handle. His response time began to suffer. The change dilemma was forced upon him against his will.

Should he now hire more subordinates, give up doing repair work himself (which is his real interest), and become a manager of a growing firm? Or should he not hire anyone else and take the risk of losing his reputation, as he would either have to refuse to service some requests or else accept all calls but no longer give as quick service? If he did lose his reputation, this latter alternative would mean that, in the long run, he might have fewer customers than he could handle, not too many. His reputation for being too busy might mean that he would not be busy at all. How should the repairman resolve his dilemma? The pressure for change is not even of his own choosing, but forced upon him by his environment. All the adaptation and maintenance that he had wanted was to correct similar types of problems in different houses, and for the right number of customers to fill each working day.

However, the right number is an almost impossible target. Because each organization deals normally with an uncountable public, demand is difficult to forecast. No organization, be it a charity, a bread manufacturer, or a repairman, wants too little demand. Change is required usually to increase demand toward the desired target, but the change brings different reactions from old users, new users, employees, and managers. It is a fortunate organization that can establish its own targets.

In the resolution of this change dilemma, of this dilemma of adaptive versus maintenance mechanisms, there is no minimum standard legislated by any nation as there were in this chapter's previous dilemmas. The minimum is merely the continued existence versus the demise of the organization (although, if the organization is important enough to the nation, some nations will subsidize its existence so that it does not die). However, the resolution still calls for compromise, not domination nor integration.

Domination of either the maintenance mechanism or the adaptive mechanism is an untenable situation which soon kills the organization. The organization dies either of lethargy or over-exertion. Too much change can be as harmful as too little. Too little growth leaves one stunted; too much, cancerous.

Integration is also not a viable resolution for the dilemma. It is not that the organization wants to find a resolution above and beyond the present goals, as integration promises. It is that the organization wants a resolution that gives it both of the present goals. Compromise is the solution. Some emphasis must be given to the maintenance mechanism, some to the adaptive. The question, as always, is — how much?

Combining the two needs within the same personnel is one type of compromise. This is rational for situations where one person has virtual control, such as teachers, lecturers, dentists, ministers. However, the compromise is not always well balanced. For example, patients often lose confidence in the general practitioner whose office, equipment, and habits reflect his graduation prior to World War II. However, they look equally askance at the overly-adaptive new doctor whose office is refurbished constantly with tons of new equipment which never appears to be used, but whose cost has to be reflected in their bills. This type of compromise is a possibility to work towards, however.

But for most organizations, the two mechanisms cannot be combined within the same personnel without creating other problems. The efficiency of production lines, for example, cannot tolerate the inclusion of the responsibility for adaptation, nor can the battery of clerks processing applications, and nor can the cashiers in the supermarket. The responsibility for change and adaptation must be assigned to someone else in these and like situations. The best the organization can hope for in these situations is some measure of tolerance between those who are maintaining the organization and those who are adapting it. The ship must be steered carefully through the dilemma.

Notes

1. E.g., Friedrich A. Hayek, 'The Corporation in a Democratic Society: in Whose Interest Ought It and Will It Be Run?' in *Management and Corporations 1985*, ed. by Melvin Anshen and George Leland Bach (New York: McGraw-Hill, 1960), pp. 99–117.
2. E.g., A. A. Berle, Jr., 'The Corporation in a Democratic Society,' in *Management and Corporations 1985*, pp. 63–98.
3. Peter Drucker, *Managing for Results* (New York: Harper & Row, 1964), p. 5.
4. A. W. Johnson, 'Efficiency in Government and Business,' *Canadian Public Administration* VI (September, 1963), 245–60.

CHAPTER 6

Epilogue

At various times during the twentieth century, it has been suggested that administration should be studied in the same manner as medicine. Since the two practices have not been studied in the same manner, the intent of the advice has been that administration should be studied like medicine, not vice versa. That is, would-be doctors do not study courses called 'medicine,' but instead study all the fields that comprise the practice — biology, anatomy, chemistry, physics, and others. Similarly, would-be administrators should study economics, psychology, computer science, statistics, law, *et al.* There should be no courses called 'administration.'

The advice misses a very important point. Although both medicine and administration are fields which encompass many different branches of knowledge, they do not do so with the same intent. Medicine has no synthesis courses called 'medicine' because it is not synthesis but analysis that leads to the improved health of a patient. The doctor analyzes the patient's malady, sifts through the symptoms, and determines cause-and-effect. The doctor then recommends the treatment that has the best effect in overcoming the cause. To the extent that there are side-effects of the remedy, the doctor must be aware of synthesis, of ensuring that the total person is improved by the treatment. However, this is normally only of importance in the treatment, not the determination of the problem. In the study of medicine, analysis is far more important than synthesis.

But this is not so in the study of administration. For the administrator or manager, synthesis takes priority over analysis. It is the synthesis of the different parts, needs, and interests of the organization that dominate the work of the administrator. As well, it is the synthesis of the knowledge gained from economics, psychology, law, mathematics, sociology, *et al.* that the administrator must practice. Analysis of the problems that are present in the organization is certainly important to the administrator, but once again it is a matter of degree.

To the administrator, analysis is not nearly so important as synthesis. The best analysis in the world will come to naught if the ability to synthesize the various parts of the organization so as to implement the solution is lacking.

In medicine, the patient is a single individual who desires the remedy; in administration, the patient is a multitude of people, with different interests and different roles, who may or may not desire the solution.

Furthermore, there are no freaks in the world of organizations. In the world of medicine, assumptions can be made about the normal human being and cause-and-effect analyses can be tested against that norm. Some human beings will be freaks whose qualities and characteristics will not align with the norm, but the student of medicine will not need to devote much time to them. The normal human being is the object of study.

This is not so for the student of administration. There are no freaks amongst organizations, and thus there is no conception of a normal organization. For example, the normal human being will have a separate set of reproductive organs, but an organization may or may not have a separate staffing department, and either possibility is equally likely. As well, the heart of a human being is located within the body and has four chambers; the 'heart' of an organization may be located in a different country from its productive 'hand' or its marketing 'mouth,' and the size of that 'heart' may vary from one human being to a board of twenty to a legislature of five hundred to a Pentagon-full. Organizations come in all sizes and shapes.

Without a norm upon which to concentrate, and its consequent freaks, the student of administration and organizations must study ranges of possibilities, each possibility a viable prospect in the real world. Analysis becomes insignificant and synthesis is paramount. For example, the authoritarian manager may produce one kind of effect amongst the subordinates in one type of organization, but may well produce the opposite effect amongst the subordinates of a different type of organization. This same manager may produce a third effect if the subordinates in that first organization are changed, and the person may not even be made a manager in a fourth organization. The permutations are so great as to make cause-and-effect statements about a norm appear trivial. Without freaks, there are no norms.

The need for an holistic approach that emphasizes synthesis of the parts of the organization means that the individual dilemmas of this book must be re-examined. Throughout the chapters, each dilemma was discussed in isolation and resolutions were recommended in isolation. One cannot leave the matter there. It may well be that the recommended resolution of one dilemma is in opposition to that for another dilemma. If a manager were to be confronted by both simultaneously, it would be of little help were the two chosen solutions to be diametrically opposed. For example, it makes little sense to resolve the attitude-towards-controls dilemma through domination of internal controls if one is also going to resolve the dilemma of the locus of decision-making authority through centralization. One needs a scorecard to show all the resolutions together (see Figure 6.1).

It is in the resolutions where domination is recommended that problems of synthesis can arise. If one is choosing a particular set of goals and eschewing another set, one has to ensure that this resolution is not negated by the resolution of another dilemma that espoused the second set. Each reader should work through the scorecard and ensure that his or her chosen resolutions are holistically sound. However, it is not feasible to discuss each situation of potential conflict here. One can only caution that a succession of dominations may negate each other.

As for the compromise and integration solutions, potential conflicts between the resolutions of these dilemmas are not likely to occur. Compromises are always fluid and flexible and can be merely readjusted, while integration removes the dilemma. However, each organizational decision-maker should keep in mind the need to coordinate the resolutions, the need to synthesize one set of goals with another, the need to ensure that one answer does not create another problem.

In concluding the Introduction to the second edition of his book, *Administrative Theories and Politics*, Peter Self stated that:

the basic problems of administration in democratic societies can neither be dissolved by nostrums, whether political or managerial, nor removed by the surgeon's knife without killing the patient. This is not to deny the possibility or desirability of reform. But while reform may readjust, it will not remove the persistence of administrative 'dilemmas.' If many of these dilemmas remain in principle highly familiar, they have now to be understood in relation to a much enlarged, more complex, and more discretionary system of administration.[1]

DILEMMA	DOMINATION	COMPROMISE	INTEGRATION
LOCUS OF DECISION – MAKING AUTHORITY	X		
GEOGRAPHICAL LOCATION	X		
PROVISION OF COMMON SERVICES	X		
USE OF STAFF EXPERTISE FOR DECISION—MAKING		X	?
BUREAUCRATIC VS. FLEXIBLE		X	
POSITIONAL AUTHORITY VS. PERSONAL AUTHORITY	X		
SPAN OF CONTROL VS. NUMBER OF LEVELS		X	
UNITY OF COMMAND VS. FUNCTIONAL COMMANDS	X		
MECHANISMS OF COORDINATION	X		
USE OF A PLANNING UNIT			X
BASIS OF DEPARTMENTALIZING	X		
BASIS OF REORGANIZING	?	X	
CAREER STAFFING VS. POSITION STAFFING	?	X	
LOYALTY VS. CRITICISM		X	
INTERNAL CONTROLS VS. EXTERNAL CONTROLS	X		
LOCATION OF EVALUATION UNIT			X
LINE – ITEM BUDGET VS. PROGRAM BUDGET	X		
MANAGER'S PERSPECTIVE TOWARDS SUBORDINATES	X		
THE TIME FOR CORRECTIVE ACTION	?		X
SOCIAL RESPONSIBILITY		X	
PARTICIPATION		X	
PROFESSIONALS		X	
EFFICIENCY		X	
CHANGE		X	
WHERE X = RECOMMENDED RESOLUTION ? = VIABLE ALTERNATIVE			

Figure 6.1 Summary of dilemmas

This statement is a fitting summary of the sentiments behind this book, too.

However, no organizational decision-maker should hide behind the persistence of dilemmas and make no decisions to resolve them. One cannot just throw up one's arms in dismay and say that it is impossible to act. To make no decision is still a decision that will leave things in a certain manner.

On the contrary, it should now be even easier for the decision-maker to choose. Modern dilemmas are merely a choice between equally likely or desirable outcomes. As long as the decision-maker can justify the outcome that is desired, the decision to achieve it is simple and straightforward. One knows in advance what one will receive.

There is a sign that one often sees at the desk of a lower-level clerk in an organization, a clerk with a wry sense of humour that is. The sign states: 'There is no reason for this; it's just our policy.' Presumably, one is expected to be amused at the amount of 'red tape' and 'bureaucracy' that must pervade that organization.

Actually, the statement on the sign is much more mature, realistic, and reasonable than might be thought. In dealing with dilemmas, it is expressing the proper sentiment perfectly. The sign might not seem as humorous, but it could just as well be written: 'The only reason for this is that we have decided to make it our policy.' That is total justification in itself.

In dealing with at least a half of the dilemmas, one must choose one set of goals or the other with no better reason than that is what one has decided to do. If one wants the goals associated with the centralization of decision-making authority, for example, one need not apologize for that desire or that choice.

It may be that the passage of time or pressures from lower-level employees or demands from the community may cause the decision-maker to compromise or to reverse that original choice and now seek the goals associated with the other prong of the dilemma. Again, one need not apologize for that. The world is constantly in a state of flux and what is necessary today may not be needed tomorrow. Perhaps the only advice that should be given for resolving dilemmas is:

'Things maun aye be someway.'

Note

1. Self, *Administrative Theories*, p. 16.

Index